# Birder's
## GUIDE TO
# ALABAMA &
# MISS...

D1463008

# Birder's GUIDE TO ALABAMA & MISSISSIPPI

## Ray Vaughan

Illustrations by Gail D. Luckner

Gulf Publishing Company
Houston, Texas

Gulf Publishing Company
Book Division
P.O. Box 2608, Houston, Texas 77252-2608

10 9 8 7 6 5 4 3 2 1

**Library of Congress Cataloging-in-Publication Data**

Vaughan, Ray.
    Birder's guide to Alabama & Mississippi / Ray Vaughan ; illustrations by Gail Diane Luckner.
        p.   cm.
    Includes index.
    ISBN 0-88415-055-0
    1. Bird watching—Alabama—Guidebooks. 2. Bird watching—Mississippi—Guidebooks. 3. Birds—Alabama. 4. Birds—Mississippi. I. Title. II. Title: Birder's guide to Alabama and Mississippi.
QL684.A2V38  1993
598′.07234761—dc20                                    93-28721
                                                           CIP

*To my beautiful wife, Louise,*
*who is my birding companion*
*and my inspiration.*

# Contents

# Acknowledgments

I would like to thank my wife, Louise, for putting up with all my trips and my worrying about this book and about the birds. Much thanks to Julia Starr and all the folks at Gulf Publishing for making this book possible. Thanks to all the birders who helped me in many small ways and who shared some birding experiences with me. Special thanks to Larry Gardella for his help and advice. Appreciation goes to Ned Mudd and Joyce Hudson, my guides on the Cahaba.

# Foreword

Traveling birders, even when they are not traveling for the express purpose of watching birds, need advice and directions that are highly specific to find good local birding spots in unfamiliar territory. How frustrating it is to drive, guideless, through a state, knowing that one is probably missing wanted species and nearby birding sites.

Of course, most bird-seekers have on hand one or several field guides, as well as books of broad use such as Olin S. Pettingill's classic eastern and western bird-finding guides or William and Laura Riley's *Guide to the National Wildlife Refuges*. Excellent bird-finding guidebooks also exist for many states and local areas, and if one has done some advance planning, these books can enhance enormously the pleasure of travel through an area.

Alabama and Mississippi contain birding locations that birders often neglect or underestimate. Now, for resident and visitor alike, Ray Vaughan's *Birders' Guide to Alabama and Mississippi* provides exactly the kind of information needed to make the most of birding opportunities in these two states. The book's explicit directions (at "mile 175.6 [a] short trail leads through a tupelo/bald cypress swamp") and maps and its detailed advice on what to look for in all seasons ("prothonotary warbler is a regular here during the spring and summer") make finding birds in these states much easier and certainly more likely. This is especially true for such elusive specialties as rails, wood storks, and red-cockaded woodpeckers. (A separate chapter lists the most sought after species in Alabama and Mississippi and the best spots to try for them.)

As Mr. Vaughan, an environmental attorney, reminds us, both Alabama and Mississippi have suffered grievous habitat destruction and degradation, and much needs to be done to preserve their remaining wild places. Even though the purpose of the *Birder's Guide to Alabama and Mississippi* is to enhance personal birding experiences, it can only lead its users to a deeper appreciation of what is at stake and will therefore surely contribute to arresting further losses and to protecting declining species.

From Mobile Bay to the Natchez Trace, bird-watchers will find Mr. Vaughan's guide to seeing both resident and migrant bird species invaluable. His book should lead to new adventures and wider horizons for those who visit Alabama and Mississippi, and for those who live there.

Mary Beacom Bowers, Editor
*Bird Watcher's Digest*

# About the Author

Ray Vaughan is an environmental lawyer, writer, and birder. His articles have appeared in *The Alabama Environmental Law Reporter, Alabama Law Review,* and *Bird Watcher's Digest,* among other publications. He has written the *Birder's Guide to Alabama & Mississippi* to bring public attention to the great birding opportunities in these two states, as well as the fact that much of the habitat is being lost because it is unprotected.

# Introduction

 Alabama and Mississippi represent the heart of what some call the Deep South, and many people think that these two states are uniform, flat stretches of pine forest and cotton fields sweltering under the heat and humidity of an endless summer. However, these states have a large variety of landforms and ecosystems that provide habitats for a wide range of plants, animals, fish, and birds. For instance, Alabama has more listed endangered and threatened species under the Endangered Species Act than any other state except for Florida and California. The area is a major portion of the migration routes for many species of birds that summer in the northern portion of the United States and winter in the tropics. While you can find cotton fields and pine plantations baking in the summer heat, there is much more to these two states.

This book is written as a useful guide to birders, helping people to see that Alabama and Mississippi are not just places to drive through when going to Texas or Florida. Alabama and Mississippi are excellent final destinations for bird-watching trips and can also make great additions to a tour of Texas or Florida. This book includes all the national forests and national wildlife refuges, many of the state parks, several city parks, and some private lands that are open to the public for birding. While this book is meant to provide

1

a variety of good birding locations to visit throughout these two states, it is by no means a complete guide to the bird-watching spots available in Alabama and Mississippi. This book is not an attempt to compile all of the birding locations in these states, nor should the locations profiled here be considered as the only good places to bird in Alabama and Mississippi. For the traveler, this book should give guidance to some of the best, most accessible, and most representative of the birding locations here. For those who move to or live in Alabama and Mississippi, this book should be considered as a beginning guide to the places to go. For someone who lives here or who spends a great deal of time here, there is no substitute for getting involved in local birding clubs and groups; the experience of those familiar with an area can guide one to the many, many birding spots that just cannot be covered by a book of this scope.

While the spots covered in this book provide excellent birding opportunities, a sad fact about these two states is that much of the habitat for birds is not publicly owned; Mississippi and Alabama, in particular, have done very little to protect the remaining wild places needed for many species of birds to survive. Currently, huge tracts of hardwood forests in northern Alabama are being logged and the wood is being cut into chips for shipment to Japan and Korea. Millions of acres of prime songbird nesting habitat will be destroyed over the next two decades, and the State of Alabama is doing nothing to prevent it; indeed, the government is encouraging this destruction of forests, some of which have remained undisturbed for a century or more. Birds such as American redstarts, ovenbirds, and many other woodland warblers are in serious decline due to this loss of habitat, very little of which is preserved in state and federal lands. Basically, the elected and appointed officials of these two states have not taken the long-term view on protection of the environment. In 1991, Alabama was ranked 50th in the nation in protecting the environment by the *1991–92 Green Index,* published by the Southern Studies Institute; Mississippi was ranked 47th. Such lack of environmental preservation makes the places that remain all the more precious. The small size of many of the areas profiled here and the large distances between these birding spots show just how much has already been lost. I hope that this book will increase the public's knowledge of what we still have in Alabama and Mississippi and that people will work to protect more of these two special states.

## ALABAMA

Alabama has an abundance of unique geologic regions and wildlife habitats; this is where the Appalachian mountain range ends. Many birds have the very southern end of their summer nesting range in the mountains of northeastern Alabama; these include the black-throated green warbler and the sharp-shinned hawk. According to a number of biologists, botanists, and other scientists, the unique geology of Alabama gives the state a diversity of species unlike any other in the nation. So little has been done on finding the species of animals, plants, fish, and insects that live in Alabama that most of the species here have never been cataloged. Some scientists theorize that, outside of the tropical rainforests of the world, Alabama has a greater diversity of species than anywhere else on the planet. With Alabama being solidly in the middle of the southern habitat of eastern birds, the state has great variety of bird species, but it still does not compare to Texas; no state does. The Alabama Bird Records Committee officially recognizes 403 species of birds as having occurred in Alabama. Most of the biological diversity in

Alabama is in those species who do not have the mobility of birds, such as salamanders, mussels, turtles, insects, plants, and fish. Alabama has a rich avian fauna, but for many other forms of life, Alabama is absolutely unique. An excellent book about birds in Alabama is available from The University of Alabama Press; *Alabama Birds*, by Thomas A. Imhof, covers the life histories of bird species known to occur in Alabama. That book is not a guidebook to birding locations, but it does tell where certain species have been spotted in the state. The main limitation of that book is that it is updated only through its 1976 edition; sighting data is almost entirely pre-1970, and some things are outdated. For example, the house finch is listed as "hypothetical"; today, that bird is everywhere in the towns and cities of Alabama. The address of the University Press is The University of Alabama Press, P.O. Drawer 2877, University, AL 35486. The book is a large hardback with color plates.

Bird habitat in Alabama runs from mountain cliffs to shoreline. In between are countless swamps, marshes, pine barrens, pitcher plant bogs, various hardwood forests, canyons, streams, rivers, lakes, grasslands, and fields. Alabama has many large rivers and lakes that attract wintering loons, ducks, geese, and bald eagles. Spring brings migration of many species of songbirds, and summer provides ample opportunity to sight such things as prothonotary and hooded warblers in the swamps, if you can stand the heat, humidity, and insects.

The Alabama Ornithological Society has been active since 1952 in observing birds and assisting birders in Alabama. If you live in Alabama, joining the AOS will give you access to the knowledge and guidance of the top birders in the state. The AOS also operates a statewide Rare Bird Hotline that one can call to receive the latest on unique birds sighted in

Alabama; the number is 205-987-2730. For more information about the AOS, the address is 803 Queen City Ave., Tuscaloosa, AL 35401.

## MISSISSIPPI

Although lacking in the variety of geologic landforms that Alabama has, Mississippi does not lack in bird variety, and the state is blessed with wetlands in abundance. Being on the Mississippi River and along the Mississippi flyway, the state's wetlands provide unparalleled opportunities for observing waterfowl. The duck life in some of Mississippi's refuges can be quite lavish and plentiful. Unfortunately, much of this wetland habitat has been converted to pine plantations and open farmland, but still, some wonderful areas remain.

A good book on birds and birding locations along the Mississippi coast is *Birds and Birding on the Mississippi Coast,* written by Judith Toups and Jerome Jackson and published by the University Press of Mississippi. Their book goes into explicit particulars about birding locations in Hancock, Harrison, and Jackson Counties; as the purpose of this book is to give a general guide to the more accessible public areas for bird watching over a two-state area, I do not attempt to get as specific on the covered areas along the Mississippi coast. However, I have included the areas that I think will be the most productive for birds and the most accessible to the traveler. For those who wish to spend more time birding along the Mississippi coast or for those who live there, *Birds and Birding on the Mississippi Coast* is highly recommended. The book is hardbound and retails for around twenty dollars; the address for the publisher is: University Press of Mississippi, Jackson, MS 39211.

A hotline for rare bird sightings along the Mississippi coast is available. That number is 601-467-9500.

## BIRDING IN THE DEEP SOUTH

The legend of the South as being hot and humid is certainly true during the summer, which is rather long. Unless there is a unique cool spell, I do not recommend going on any strenuous birding activities during the summer here. There are plenty of easily accessible locations where one can bird without arduous walking, such as along the beach or in areas easily accessible from your car. A long walk in the woods or swamps can be a miserable, even deadly, thing during the summer in Alabama and Mississippi. The heat and humidity really do reach epic proportions from late May through early September; heatstroke and heat exhaustion can overwhelm the unprepared person who takes to the woods.

Further, the poison ivy, mosquitoes, ticks, and chiggers are ubiquitous during the summer. Although rarely seen by most people, poisonous snakes such as a variety of rattlesnake species, copperhead, water moccasin, and coral snake all live down here; watch where you step and where you put your hands when in the woods and swamps. Also, particularly when in fields, one must watch out for fire ants; their gang attacks and multiple stings can be a danger, but if you do not disturb their mounds, they will leave you alone. Another summer danger that is relatively insignificant but must be considered anyway in these states is the American alligator. In marshes and swamps in the southern parts of both states, alligators have made a good comeback, and they do live in the kinds of habitats that make for good birding. Since they can be in any wet area, watch for them; they do not want to deal with people and will usually stay out of your way.

Seeing nesting hooded and prothonotary warblers deep in a swamp has been my reward for hard-core birding during the summer in Alabama, but I do not plan to do that again, as there are easier places to find such birds. Unless you are at the beach or in the mountains of northeastern Alabama, where it is surprisingly much cooler, I do not recommend birding most of the areas of Alabama and Mississippi during the summer months if any significant walking is involved. Stay off the major trails and try those places that are accessible by car.

However, what cruelties Alabama and Mississippi impose during the summers are redeemed by the pleasant winters. While much of the country is frozen, these states provide what can be some of the finest winter birding anywhere. The temperatures are moderate; the bugs and poison ivy are gone, and many northern bird species find this area a great place to spend the winter. Hiking through the southern woods in winter is as comfortable as being outdoors can ever be, and winter can bring you birds as diverse as common loons, ducks, numerous sparrow species, and bald eagles. Often a light jacket or a sweater is all you will need for warmth. The only drawback to winter birding in Alabama and Mississippi is that on certain lands, particularly the national forests, you will have to compete with hunters for use of the woods. During hunting seasons, other areas such as state parks and certain wildlife refuges make safer places to bird. Although it is a rare occurrence, winter storms with dangerous ice and snow do occur here, but such events are so infrequent as to be major news. Even cursory reviews of the weather reports will alert you to one of these rare storms.

Spring and autumn are great seasons for birding, as prime migration routes for many species are in Alabama and Mississippi. Spring along the Gulf coast can bring a wealth of songbird species, and early fall at Mobile Bay is the staging area for the southern migration of terns, sometimes numbering in the thousands at one time. Waterfowl that winter in South America can put on spring migration displays that are truly awesome; groupings of up to 100,000 lesser scaup have been seen off the shores of Alabama, and large gatherings of ducks along the wetlands of the Mississippi flyway in Mississippi can be equally impressive.

The birding rewards can be great in these two states; just use common sense and be prepared for any possibilities in weather, plants, insects, or terrain. Although inconvenient, and occasionally dangerous to humans, the bothersome life forms of the deep South are indicators of the great diversity of life here.

# Alabama

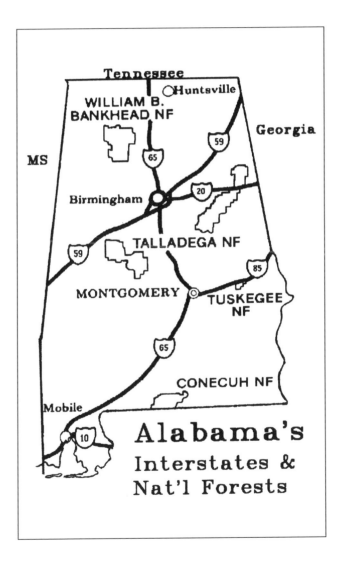

Tennessee

○Huntsville

WILLIAM B.
BANKHEAD NF

Georgia

59

MS

65

Birmingham

20

TALLADEGA NF

59

85

MONTGOMERY

TUSKEGEE
NF

65

CONECUH NF

Mobile

10

## Alabama's
### Interstates &
### Nat'l Forests

# Chapter 1
# Coastal Alabama

## DAUPHIN ISLAND

 Dauphin Island is undoubtedly the mecca for birding in Alabama. If you bird only one place in Alabama, most people would agree that this island must be that place. Here is where huge numbers of migrants come through both in the spring and in autumn; also, many accidentals have been seen on Dauphin Island. With a large variety of bird habitats for a barrier island, this place can provide endless birding opportunities year-round. All of the prime sites for bird-watching are easily accessible, and the local citizenry has gotten used to seeing people with binoculars and cars moving very slowly along the quiet streets of the town.

Dauphin Island is reached by two routes. One can drive directly to the island by taking SH 193 south from I-10, at exit 17A, west of Mobile. SH 193 will turn to the east and then resume its southward route to the island; a formerly direct route from Mobile is no longer possible due to a washed-out bridge. US 193 will head south along the western edge of Mobile Bay and then will cross Mississippi Sound over a large bridge to the island. Stopping on the bridge is not allowed and is unsafe, but if you stop prior to

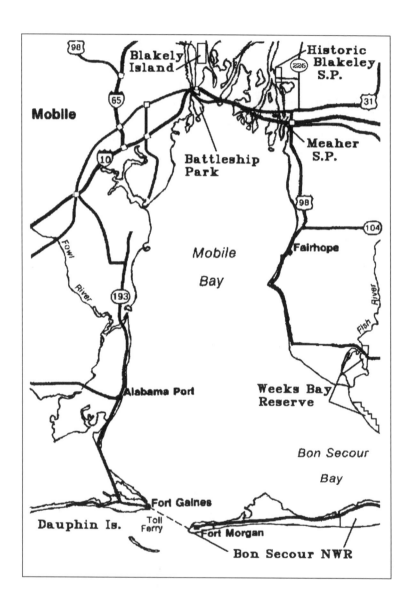

getting on the bridge at the Cedar Point Fishing Pier, look out to the southwest at the series of sand bars in the Sound. You will often see a variety of wading birds. In particular, look for black skimmers. Often, there is a group of white pelicans that likes to hang out on one particular sandbar. Once you are on Dauphin Island, SH 193 will pass the docks and several stores and then dead-end into Bienville Boulevard, which is the main east-west road along the spine of the island. Stopping in the area of the docks can give views of the sandbars in the nearby waters, and often wading birds and shore birds can be seen there. The other way to reach the island is to take the ferry from Fort Morgan.

Dauphin Island represents the best spot in Alabama to catch what is known as a "fallout" during the spring migration; during the spring months, a storm or strong low pressure center may make extra difficulty for the birds migrating across the Gulf of Mexico. When these conditions occur, the birds that survive the journey will land and collect on the first piece of suitable land that they encounter upon reaching the mainland. Then those birds will remain at that site longer than usual in order to eat, rest, and regain their strength for their northward voyage. Although many birds will stop once they reach first land, they may not stop for long if they are in good shape; thus a storm over the Gulf can mean a great number of essentially exhausted birds which congregate at first landfall. Although this gathering of weary and resting birds can be a bonanza for the birder, it is tragic for the birds, because such storms mean that many birds will not survive the migration across the Gulf and that the ones that do have a reduced chance of survival on the rest of their journey.

Many migrating birds make Dauphin Island their first landfall after crossing the Gulf, and when there is a fallout, the island can be practically covered with birds that make little attempt to hide, flee, or even get out of the road for cars. Even without a fallout, though, Dauphin Island birding in the spring can be spectacular. One minute you can be standing under a tree with nothing in it, and a moment later, a hundred warblers of six or seven different species will land in that tree. During good days, one can see dozens of species of warblers and vireos and hundreds of individuals of some species. On one late March day, I saw over four hundred black-and-white warblers within four hours on Dauphin Island. Basically, any warbler that migrates from the tropics to central and eastern North America can be seen on Dauphin Island, but for some of the rarer species, it is still a matter of luck. It is impossible to predict the best time to visit during the spring; conditions and the number of birds can fluctuate from hour to hour.

Although many bird watchers claim that early to mid-April is best for spring migration on Dauphin Island, I have had the best luck during the last week of March for warblers, while April has been better for me for buntings, orioles, tanagers, and dickcissels. From late March to late April marks the majority of the spring migration, and if you can visit on more than one day, your chances of seeing a great number of birds and a large variety of species rises substantially. Other species that are often seen during the spring include rose-breasted grosbeak, veery, wood thrush, Louisiana waterthrush, northern waterthrush, blue grosbeak, northern oriole, orchard oriole, scarlet tanager, summer tanager, indigo bunting, painted bunting, various species of flycatchers, eastern kingbird, yellow-billed cuckoo, and black-billed cuckoo.

During the summer, magnificent frigatebirds can sometimes be seen out in the Gulf to the south of Dauphin

*Painted Bunting*

Island. Sighting one from shore is rare, but a trip out on a boat will greatly increase one's chances of sighting one. Gray kingbirds are also summer residents. In late summer, reddish egret can occasionally be found, particularly on the shores along Mississippi Sound.

Fall migration is more spaced out, depending upon the type of birds involved. Terns, particularly black terns, will begin their migration as early as July; the mouth of Mobile Bay is a major staging area for black terns in their migration to South America, and thousands at one time can sometimes be encountered. Southward songbird migration is more spread-out than spring migration north, and so any time from late summer through autumn may provide you with a good day of birding. Many of the later migrants are ducks. During the winter, Dauphin Island is an excellent place to find many wintering birds, including mergansers, common loon, red-breasted nuthatch, eared grebe, horned grebe, and palm warbler. Often, the common loons will not leave until April. Arctic loon and red-throated loon are rare winter visitors to the island.

The island has a number of hot spots, and if one is not very productive at a particular time, then you can easily travel to another place and check out the action there.

The island is also a magnet for accidentals. Northern goshawk, scissor-tailed flycatcher, groove-billed ani, western tanager, black-whiskered vireo, shiny cowbird (which is increasing its presence in the area) and many other species rare for this region have been sighted here.

**Shell Mounds**

This is a small plot of land that hosts an inordinately large amount of bird activity, and it is the prime spot on Dauphin Island for birding. Managed by the Alabama Department of Conservation and Natural Resources, the Shell Mounds are an ancient Native American site where discarded oyster shells were piled up to such an extent that a series of small hills were created. To reach the Shell Mounds, turn north off of Bienville Boulevard onto Iberville Drive 0.5 mile east of SH 193; the Shell Mounds are two blocks down Iberville Drive. If there is nowhere to park near the entrance, the road winds around the eastern side of the mounds, and additional parking can be found there and on the northern side.

The mounds are covered with brush and trees, some quite large, and the swales between the mounds are mostly grassy. For such a small area, there are dozens of trails winding through the trees and the mounds, and one can take a very twisting course through this area. All these trails are there to allow many birders as much access to the area as possible, because the density of birds at this one location can be so high at times that every bush will bring new discoveries.

Spring is definitely the hottest birding season at the Shell Mounds. I have stood in one spot and looked at one tree, and within two minutes I saw the following warblers: northern parula, yellow-throated, Blackburnian, prothonotary, black-and-white, yellow-rumped, hooded, and blue-winged. Warblers, vireos, and orioles are some of the biggest prizes to be found at the Shell Mounds, but concentration on the bushes and trees should not keep you from looking up beyond the trees occasionally. Peregrine falcon, merlin, Cooper's hawk, red-shouldered hawk, swallow-tailed kite, Mississippi kite, osprey, American kestrel, and other birds of prey have often been seen flying over the Shell Mounds, sometimes just above tree level. Once I saw a Cooper's hawk fly through the trees on the northern end of the mounds. Peregrines can sometimes be seen flying high overhead during migration, and there are a few of the falcons that reside along Alabama's Gulf coast.

Ruby-throated hummingbirds will gather in the dozens among the honeysuckle and other flowers in the field at the southern end of the mounds. Orioles and tanagers can also be found, sometimes in great abundance, in the same area. Warblers and vireos can be found anywhere throughout the mounds, and with their interest in feeding after their trans-Gulf flight, many are often unconcerned about the numerous people around them. During one April trip, I was able to stand still and watch a half-dozen hooded warblers hunt through the leaves at my feet. Indigo buntings gather in the dozens, particularly during the later part of spring migration; watch any flocks of indigoes carefully for the occasional painted bunting that flocks with them.

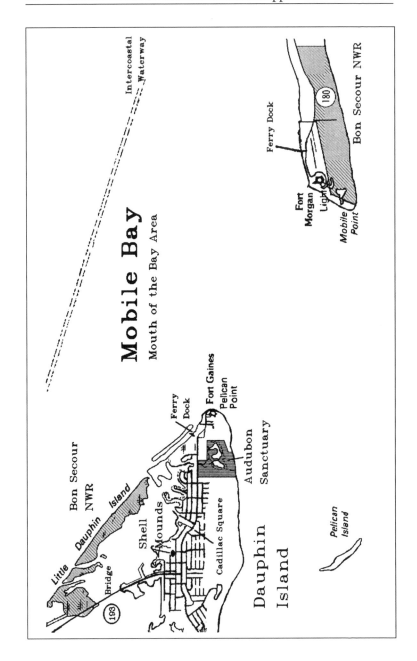

**Mobile Bay**
Mouth of the Bay Area

There is a bird sightings reporting box at the northeastern corner of the Shell Mounds. Check this box for any recent sightings on the island. While the places listed here are the main areas to bird on the island, anywhere can have good sightings; so check the listings for other spots where unusual species have been sighted.

## Audubon Sanctuary

Three-tenths of a mile west of the ferry dock is an area managed by the Mobile Bay Audubon Society. Many trails run through the pine and oak woodlands that attract large numbers of migrants. There is also a beautiful, spring-fed lake (rare for a barrier island) that has regular herons and alligators. A large swamp is also part of this sanctuary.

The trail that loops around the lake, through the swamps and wooded dunes, and then through the banding area provides the best variety of habitats for spotting migrants. The banding area and the woods just south of it are often very productive. One overhanging oak tree on the very northern face of the dunes can also be a fertile area for warblers and vireos. An area dominated by a very large magnolia tree with a bench underneath it can be very productive for warblers, as well. A viewing stand overlooks part of the swamp; during spring, this is a good spot for prothonotary warbler, northern waterthrush, red-eyed vireo, and green-backed heron. On rare occasions, such as in spring of 1992, black-whiskered vireos have been seen in this swampy area near the stand.

At the southern end of the sanctuary, there is a boardwalk that goes out into the dunes and down to the rapidly eroding beach of Dauphin Island. During spring migration, the dunes are a good area to see migrating warblers make their first landfall, sometimes in groups of several hundred. Loons can often be seen as late as April, cruising the waves just off-shore at this point. The usual array of shorebirds and terns and gulls can be seen here. In mid-March of 1992, I witnessed over 100,000 ducks, almost entirely lesser scaup, amass in the waters off this beach between Dauphin Island and the Sand Island lighthouse, visible about 2 miles offshore. The ducks were gathered on the water, and when new waves of migrants high in the sky arrived, the ducks on the water rose up in mas-sive clouds to join them in heading over the island to the northwest. It was a truly impressive sight.

## Fort Gaines

   Fort Gaines is a pre-Civil War era masonry fort on the very eastern tip of the island. Here are good views to the east and south over the mouth of Mobile Bay. The island is eroding very rapidly at this point, and a number of stone jetties that once were on the beach are now some distance out in the water. It is ironic that the building of these jetties was meant to prevent beach erosion, but they actually sped up the process. These jetties now provide space for shorebirds. The parking lot at the very end of the road gives you a view of these jetties; look for brown pelican, least, royal, gull-billed, Caspian, Sandwich, Forster's, and common terns, a variety of gulls, black skimmer, American oystercatcher, willet, and double-crested cormorant. In winter look at the cormorants carefully, for a few great cormorants have been known to occur here and at other areas on the Alabama coast. Poma-rine jaegers have been seen in late winter and spring.

## Cadillac Square

This historic spot on Bienville Boulevard east of the Shell Mounds and west of the Audubon Sanctuary was the capital of French Louisiana from 1710 to 1717. It is now a rest area with toilets and a picnic ground, but with its large live oaks, it can often have great numbers of migrant warblers. I have seen the square empty; then it filled with over two hundred warblers, and half an hour later, it was empty again. It is a easy place to check out when other places are cold, and it is the best place for public toilets.

## The Airport

The island's small airport is located in the middle of a large saltwater marsh on the northern side of the island. This is a good place to listen for rails, particularly clapper rail. In winter, black rail has been heard here as recently as 1992. Egrets and herons can be fairly abundant here, with tricolored heron not being unusual, and reddish egret possible. Northern harrier can commonly be seen over the marsh in winter. From the western arm of Bienville Boulevard, take Omega Street north, right, to a T-intersection where the left fork takes you immediately to the airport parking lot. Using recorded calls, I have been able to get both clapper rail and black rail to respond from the marsh on the north side of the road to the airport.

## Western End

The western arm of Bienville Boulevard passes lots of vacation homes and then dead-ends into a rather rough dirt road. From here, the western end of the island consists of private undeveloped land, but it is still heavily used by beachgoers and people in four-wheel-drive vehicles. Driving upon the sands and dunes of the western end of the island is strictly illegal, but that does not stop the abuse by these careless people. This part of the island consists of beach, very low dunes, and brackish marshes along the back side of the island. You can take as long or as short a walk as you desire in this area and spot shorebirds, waders, and other birds of the beach. Night-herons can be found in the marshy areas. During migration, certain migrants may turn up here also. Along the paved portion of the road to the western end of the island you can spot many kestrels and kingfishers on the power lines.

**General Areas**

Drive slowly along the quieter streets of the island when you are through with the major areas for birding. Often, birds such as indigo bunting, painted bunting, scarlet tanager, summer tanager, Louisiana waterthrush, and others forage in the yards of the homes on the island. Often, the best views of these birds can be had by just stopping along the road and watching them in a yard. During spring, the residents are used to people in cars driving slowly and stopping to stare at birds through binoculars.

## BON SECOUR NATIONAL WILDLIFE REFUGE

The Bon Secour National Wildlife Refuge consists of five units that total over 4,000 acres. Three of these units are inaccessible except by boat, but the two units that are readily accessible are also wonderful spots for birding. Many unique species that accidentally wander into Alabama find landfall at Fort Morgan. The fort is owned by the state, and the state's land is bordered on the east by the Fort Morgan Unit of the refuge. Here is the very western tip of Fort Morgan Peninsula, and one can easily watch birds over Mobile Bay and along the coast. If you are lucky, you can stand on the dock at the mouth of the Bay and watch dolphins pass from the gulf into the bay, or vice versa. Exploring the fort itself is an interesting way to pass a couple of hours, and its walls provide excellent vantage points for watching birds in all directions. Many times, birds in migration or rare wanderers can be seen merely resting in the grass around the fort.

Some of the rarities and unusual occasionals seen at Fort Morgan include little gull (one was seen in April 1992), white-winged dove, gray kingbird, buff-breasted sandpiper, black-whiskered vireo, scissor-tailed flycatcher, magnificent frigatebird, northern gannet, black-shouldered kite, and burrowing owl. Also being seen more often at Fort Morgan are the unwelcome shiny and bronzed cowbirds. More common migrants include the full range of migratory warblers and vireos, orioles, summer tanager, scarlet tanager, ruby-throated hummingbird, indigo bunting, painted bunting, blue grosbeak, rose-breasted grosbeak, bobolink, clay-colored sparrow, and many more. The fort is a major first stop for many different migrating birds in the spring and an important last stop in the fall.

This area consists of open, grassy fields with flowers, pine and oak woods, marshes, and bay and beach shoreline. Migrating upland sandpipers can sometimes be seen at the grassy areas. Brown pelican and various terns and gulls are regular on both shores. Double-crested cormorant can be seen on the pilings on the bay side. The beach goes from Fort Morgan to the national wildlife refuge and is an excellent place for shorebirds and various terns and gulls. Possible here in migration are semipalmated sandpiper, stilt sandpiper, and lesser golden plover. Year-round shorebird residents include snowy plover, black-bellied plover (rare in summer), American oystercatcher, and willet. Wilson's plover is an occasional summer resident. Winter brings a number of shorebirds, including piping plover, semipalmated plover, ruddy turnstone, red knot, sanderling, dunlin, least sandpiper, spotted sandpiper, and western sandpiper.

*Piping Plover*

To get to Fort Morgan and the adjacent refuge area, take SH 180 west from SH 59 in Gulf Shores; the turn is at a light and it is marked with signs pointing to the fort and to the ferry to Dauphin Island, which leaves from a dock near the fort. It is about 22 miles from Gulf Shores to the fort. Just before entering the fort area (the road crosses an old seawall), turn left on the paved road and go about 0.3 mile to the beach; this is the most direct route into the middle of the refuge unit.

The other major unit of the refuge is the largest; the Perdue unit straddles one of the wider parts of the peninsula and sits at the western end of Little Lagoon. The headquarters (with information center) for the refuge is located on SH 180 a little past mile marker 15 when coming from Gulf Shores to the east. The parking area for the trailhead into the unit is right at mile marker 12. Here, you can hike a leisurely 1.5 miles through the pine/oak forest to Little Lagoon and Alligator Lake and on through the dunes to the beach. Be prepared for biting flies and mosquitoes during the summer months in the forested area along the trail, and in the lake, there are alligators, large ones. Please stay on the trail when going through the dune area, as this is critical habitat for the endangered Alabama beach mouse (*Peromyscus polionotus ammobates*), and the least possible amount of disturbance to the dunes is necessary to protect this rare animal. The mouse also lives at the Fort Morgan unit of the refuge.

Migration in the fall begins in July and August, and though I have never seen much in the way of warblers in Bon Secour during the fall, the shorebird migration can be spectacular at that time of year. During August, the black terns can be seen in their full range of plumage from all black and gray to mottled, and in September, they can be seen by the thousands in their winter plumage. In late August and early September of 1991, the migration of terns was especially exciting at Bon Secour. In one afternoon, I counted an estimated 3,500 black terns in the Fort Morgan Unit of the refuge, along with at least 1,000 sandwich terns. This vast conglomeration of terns was feeding on a massive school of small fish that had been pushed to shore after a storm. Also among the flock were hundreds of common terns, Forster's terns, least terns, gull-billed terns, and even three dozen roseate terns. The roseate terns are rare wanderers to this area, but Hurricane Bob had just passed up the East Coast, disrupting these birds' usual migration route, and a number of fronts and storms had pushed through the country and into the Gulf. Thanks to the hurricane and other storms and the high concentration of fish, a thrilling collection of terns came together at Bon Secour in 1991.

In the swampy areas, look for marsh wren, least bittern, green-backed heron, sora, yellow rail, and king rail. Ground doves can sometimes be seen in the more inland dune areas. Wooded areas at the main unit before you reach Alligator Lake can produce Acadian flycatcher and prairie warbler during the summer.

A bird checklist with 373 species for the Bon Secour National Wildlife Refuge and other information can be obtained by writing Refuge Manager, Bon Secour National Wildlife Refuge, P.O. Box 1650, Gulf Shores, AL 35542.

## GULF STATE PARK

Definitely one of the crown jewels of Alabama, Gulf State Park preserves some of the very last beach, dune, and coastal pine forest habitats left in Alabama. Development has destroyed virtually all of the remaining areas of these three critical habitats, and this park and the Bon Secour National Wildlife Refuge are the only remaining portions. However, there is trouble even with these fragments that remain. At the time of this writing, a plan by the Retirement Systems of Alabama would develop up to 1,000 acres of Gulf State Park's forest preserve as a 54-hole golf course to attract tourists. On this land are large, old pine trees that provide habitat for the red-cockaded woodpecker, an endangered species, and for the endangered eastern indigo snake, and the rare gopher tortoise. Development of this park land as yet another golf course for the region would mean the end of the last state-owned coastal pine forest.

## Main Park Area

After crossing the intracoastal waterway on the Dr. Holmes Bridge, heading into Gulf Shores on I-59, one can reach the main, nonbeach park area by turning left (east) onto Highway 180 at the second traffic light. After 0.25 mile, turn south onto SH 135 and you will immediately enter the park. The headquarters will be on your left. Another quarter mile will bring you to a fork; SH 135 continues to the right and will take you to Lake Shelby, a picnic area on the lake, and an intersection with SH 182, which runs along the coast. The Lodge Complex is on the beach across from the intersection of SH 135 and SH 182. The left fork is Baldwin County Road 2; this will take you to the cabins on the north side of Lake Shelby, the existing golf course, the campgrounds, and an intersection with SH 182, about 0.5 mile east of the intersection of SH 135 and SH 182. The campgrounds are on Middle Lake, and they have a number of trails that go through the woods surrounding the campgrounds. Various pine woodland species such as white-eyed vireo can be found here, and luck will allow you to see one of the few red-cockaded woodpeckers that live in the park. Marshy areas along the trails, particularly along Bear Creek Trail (which starts on the northern side of the campground, close to the middle of the campground area), have produced king rail year-round and yellow rail in the winter and early spring.

Areas with younger pines can have prairie warblers. In warm weather, the insects here can be very annoying. The preserved area of pine woods is immediately east of the campgrounds and Middle Lake, and entry on foot is the only means of exploring here. Finding the red-cockaded woodpecker is a chancy proposition as the few birds have more than 1,000 acres to roam over; nonetheless, having this bird still alive in pine habitat this close to the Gulf of Mexico is unusual.

## Public Beach

Along SH 182, Gulf State Park preserves about 2 miles of beach and dunes. Various shorebirds can be seen here, and flights of brown pelicans in formation are virtually guaranteed throughout the day during almost any time of year. In late summer, collections of small fish just offshore may attract large flocks of terns of various species. Black terns, in particular, may appear here in late summer before they migrate to South America.

## Perdido Point Public Beach

Perdido Point, also known as Florida Point, is on the eastern side of the pass out of Perdido Bay at the very western end of Perdido Key. After crossing the bridge over Perdido Pass on SH 182, take an immediate right onto the access road that leads to a public parking area under, and south of, the bridge. Here there is a path that leads to a boardwalk over the dunes to the beach. The birds that can be spotted here are the same ones that can be seen at other areas along the Alabama coast; one would have no trouble seeing brown pelican, double-crested cormorant, and a variety of gulls and terns. In winter, common loon can be found inside the seawalls at the mouth of Perdido Bay. This is a nice and little-used area that provides about a mile of undeveloped beach to walk and to bird upon. Northern gannet can sometimes be seen from the jetty at the mouth of the bay.

The truly unique thing about Perdido Point is that the dunes here are critical habitat for one of the rarest creatures on Earth, the Perdido Key beach mouse (*Peromyscus polionotus trissylepsis*), a listed endangered species. Perhaps fewer than a hundred mice survive in the wild, and Perdido Point is one of only two known habitats left for this species which lives solely on Perdido Key. These mice are nocturnal; their burrows and their habit of distributing seeds of sea oats and other grasses may help stabilize the dunes. Please stay off the dunes: human foot traffic and litter harm the mice. If you stay on the main path, the boardwalk, and the beach, your presence should not impact the mice. Also, take all your garbage with you rather than placing it in the cans provided at the parking lot. The less trash there is, the slighter the attraction will be for feral cats and foxes that eat the mice, and for house mice which compete with the beach mice.

Gulf State Park has an official bird list put together by Thomas A. Imhof, the author of *Alabama Birds*. This list includes 347 species and covers the whole area known as Pleasure Island, which is the land south of the intracoastal waterway from Fort Morgan on the west to Perdido Pass on the east. This bird list and other information about the park can be obtained by writing Gulf State Park, 20115 State Highway 135, Gulf Shores, AL 36542.

## WEEKS BAY NATIONAL ESTUARINE RESERVE

Weeks Bay is a small but dynamic estuary off Bon Secour Bay, which makes up the southeastern portion of Mobile Bay; Weeks Bay is fed by the lovely Magnolia and Fish Rivers. In February of 1986, 3,028 acres of water, marsh, and woodland were set aside as the Weeks Bay National Estuarine Reserve. Much of the reserve is along the shore of Bon Secour Bay and is inaccessible except by boat; however, the portion of the reserve around the sides of Weeks Bay is a very accessible area and provides some very fine birding.

Access to Weeks Bay is found between mile markers 63 and 64 on SH 98, west of Foley. Although a visitor center is planned and it will be next to the road and very visible, currently there is only an unpaved parking lot at the trailhead. This small parking lot is located on the south side of SH 98, 0.6 miles west of the end of the L. W. "Louie" Brannan Bridge spanning the Fish River. At the parking lot is a small information center stocked with a number of pamphlets about Weeks Bay, including a booklet on the more common birds found here.

The easy trail starts out along the edge of a field and orchard where one may glimpse purple martins, eastern meadowlarks, and possibly a red-tailed hawk. The trail reaches a large live oak that has some benches and a lectern underneath it; on pleasant winter days, this oak can be filled with yellow-rumped warblers and ruby-crowned kinglets. Past the oak, the trail goes into the woods which are predominantly young pines; here, look for pine warblers and various kinds of sparrows. The trail winds through these woods and gradually enters an area with more bottomland hardwoods; then a boardwalk brings you out to the marshes along the edge of the bay.

During the winter, be very quiet as you move along the boardwalk and watch for ripples in the water in the marsh reeds below; this is probably the best spot in Alabama to find wintering Virginia rails. I have stood on this boardwalk and seen them not eight feet away; they are extremely difficult to spot in the marsh grasses, even when you know you are looking right at them. They are almost impossible to spot until one sees the ripples caused by their footsteps in the water among the reeds. Clapper rails can also be found here in the marsh year-round. Out over the bay, one can find birds such as brown pelican, double-crested cormorant, several types of herons, various egrets, osprey, laughing gull, herring gull, common tern, least tern, royal tern, and belted kingfisher. During winter, one can also see wintering hooded and red-breasted mergansers, horned grebe, and pied-billed grebe.

*Virginia Rail*

The trail continues through the marshs and woods alongside the bay; watch for common yellowthroat, swamp sparrow, and fish crow. A small dock provides a good look out into the bay, but it is in deteriorating condition. The trail turns back into the woods to eventually rejoin itself. During this last part of the trail, the hardwood trees are larger, and one can locate various woodpecker species. I have found the hairy woodpecker easy to spot here. Many of the plants along the trail are identified by small signs.

## FAIRHOPE

Located on the eastern shore of Mobile Bay, the beautiful town of Fairhope was founded in the late 1800s as a single tax colony. This experiment was based on the theory of having land ownership in common and a single tax as the source of all government funding. The thoughtful and deliberate development of Fairhope led to the lovely town that exists today, with wide streets, large oak trees, beautiful homes, and quaint shops. Also, the town preserved most of its waterfront as a public park.

Fairhope is reached by taking US 98 south from I-10 through Daphne and Montrose, then turning on Alternate 98 to get to Fairhope's downtown section. A turn to the west on the main road will bring you to the waterfront park and the town pier, which extends a full quarter mile out into Mobile Bay. This pier has a restaurant and provides fishing. It also makes a good platform from which to look for birds such as royal tern, Caspian tern, brown pelican, double-crested cormorant, least tern, and Forster's tern. Laughing gulls, ring-billed gulls, and herring gulls congregate in large numbers near the parking lot and are very domesticated such that they can be fed with bread. The park along the beach contains mallards and imported muscovy ducks, and these residents can sometimes attract other species such as white-fronted geese to stop and stay in the park. During winter, common loons can be readily seen just off the pier, diving for fish. The pier and beach park also provide excellent places to watch the sunset over the bay.

## BATTLESHIP PARK

Off the causeway east of Mobile over Mobile Bay is Battleship Park, home of the retired navy battleship U.S.S. *Alabama*. The park is an obvious feature off US 90/98, and there is an exit off I-10 for the park. At the southwest corner of the parking lot, there is a concrete walkway that goes out through a field to the west. This is the Pinto Pass Nature Observatory. The trail leads to a boardwalk that goes out over the marsh, and there is an observation tower at the end of the boardwalk. This tower provides a view south into the bay and a good view to the west of part of Mobile's industrial waterfront. In the bay to the south is a small island; dozens of white pelicans sometimes congregate here; bring a spotting scope to get a good view of them.

Some of the birds that can be seen here include black skimmer, various tern species, various gulls, seaside sparrow, brown pelican, white ibis, black-crowned night-heron, yellow-crowned night-heron, snowy egret, great egret, green-backed heron, tricolored heron, and great blue heron. Look for rails in the marsh grasses. Although this is a small area, this park can produce some good surprises. In recent winters, long-billed curlews have been seen at the park. Marbled godwit and upland sandpiper have also been seen, particularly during spring. I spotted two long-billed curlews in February, 1992, in the field north of the parking lot for the battleship. This field can also have large numbers of gulls, western sandpipers, red knots, killdeer, and some fish crows.

*Long-billed Curlew*

In addition to the battleship, the park contains a submarine, a B-52 bomber, and a number of other, smaller planes and navy equipment. This is a good place to combine a visit to historic war machines with some birding.

## BLAKELY ISLAND

As a large, somewhat polluted industrial area, Blakely Island seems an unlikely place to bird, but the state-owned portion of this island in Mobile is a wonderful birding spot. The state docks department controls the northern end of Blakely Island, and this area is a series of diked ponds used as a disposal site for dredging wastes and for various types of wastewater. Because the property is an active industrial site, its character and its suitability for birds changes regularly. However, due to its large size, there are usually several ponds within the facility that have had time to revegetate and become suitable for the birds that gather there.

Blakely Island is the one spot in Alabama and Mississippi where black-necked stilt is virtually guaranteed to be seen, as a large number nest here. Mottled duck is also a breeder here. Wintering ducks gather by the hundreds and often linger well into early spring; northern shoveler, green-winged teal, blue-winged teal, American coot, and mottled duck can be sighted on several lakes. Wading birds that occur here include the aforementioned black-necked stilt, lesser yellowlegs, American avocet, and glossy ibis. Spring migrants can include stilt sandpiper, white-rumped sandpiper, solitary sandpiper, and marbled godwit in the ponds, and warblers in the trees and brush along the southwestern portion of the property. Various egrets are usually present. Watch the skies overhead for merlin that patrol the ponds during winter and early spring. Painted buntings nest in some of the brush along the dikes. In winter, yellow-rumped and palm warblers can be found in the brush.

Blakely Island is an active industrial area and no facilities are provided for visitors; there are no restrooms. Indeed, for a number of years, Blakely Island was closed to birders and all visitors. Only recently has the state agreed to allow birders back on the property, and a special permit must be obtained prior to visiting the site. To get a permit, write to: General Manager, Administration, Alabama State Docks Department, P.O. Box 1588, Mobile, AL 36633; fill out page one of the permit and return it to that address. Retain page two, as it contains the rules you must abide by, and you must place it on the dashboard of your car when you are visiting the facility. You must notify the state at least one day

*Black-necked Stilt*

prior to your visit; call the Protection Unit of the Alabama State Docks at 205-690-6082 and tell them the time of your visit, the number of people, and the type of vehicle you have. You can gain access to the property only on foot, and you must stay on the established roads. As an active industrial site, Blakely Island presents some real danger to anyone who ventures onto areas where they should not go. Please obey all requirements, because the ability of other birders to visit the site depends on your maintaining good relations with the state docks department during your visit.

To reach the facility, take exit 27 off I-10, east of Mobile, and east of the tunnel under the river. Go north on the road designated as U.S. Highways Truck West 90 and 98. At 2 miles and 2.2 miles, there will be gated dirt roads to the east (right) that lead up to the top of a dike; these are the two access points to the facility. If you reach the large bridge that turns west and goes over the river, you are leaving Blakely Island and have gone too far. There is very little parking space at either entrance; the northernmost one does have slightly better parking. Pull off the highway, but make sure that you do not block access to the gates and the roads. Walk up the road to the top of the dike, and you will then be able to see over most of the facility. Follow the roads along the tops of the dikes to reach the various ponds and lakes. During 1992, the lakes on the northern end of the facility were being used and had little bird life; the lakes in the middle and somewhat toward the southern end were the prime spots for birds at that time.The opposite was the case in 1993.

Be prepared for mosquitoes, gnats, flies, and other bugs and for hot weather throughout most of the year. Be ready to walk two or more miles in order to see the birds. A spotting scope will be very useful to you, and you may be able to find a spot on a dike between two ponds that will give you views of much of the wildlife without having to move.

## MOBILE-TENSAW RIVERS DELTA

Where the Alabama and Tombigbee Rivers come together north of Mobile, a huge inland delta is formed; this 250,000-acre area is bounded by the Tensaw River on the east and the Mobile River on the west. Along and between these two rivers is a maze of watery bayou passages that surround the most remote and least developed hardwood bottomlands in Alabama. Except for Interstate 65, a power line, and a railroad line, the only human structures in the delta are fishing and hunting cabins. Most of the delta is owned by large timber companies and they are steadily clearcutting much of this incredible treasure, but due to the work of the Coastal Land Trust and the Nature Conservancy, some of the delta is being preserved.

Although the delta contains large amounts of good habitat for water birds and for nesting swamp birds, getting into the delta to see the birds can be difficult. Driving down Interstate 65 toward Mobile will give you a good view of the delta, but stopping along the highway is strictly impossible. A boat is the only practical way to explore the delta, and chartering a boat is beyond the means of many birders. However, Wildland Expeditions' boat *Gator Bait* does take people on two-hour excursions into part of the delta from the Chickasaw Marina. More information about these trips can be had by calling 205-460-8206. As of this writing, trips were being provided year-round at 9:00 a.m. and 2:00 p.m., Wednesday through Sunday. The Chickasaw Marina is located on SH 43, just south of the intersection with SH 158, two miles east of I-65, exit 13.

For those who wish to see the delta from the land, there are a couple of easily accessible points that will give you a chance to see both the forested portion and the sawgrass habitat at the southern end of the delta where it meets Mobile Bay.

## HISTORIC BLAKELEY STATE PARK

Located on the eastern side of the Tensaw River, Historic Blakeley State Park preserves an important Civil War battlefield in Alabama. However, the 3,800 acres of this park also provide good birding in the woods that are part of the delta. The park is on SH 225, about 6 miles north of Interstate 10, exit 35 (the SH 31 exit) and is 16 miles south of I-65, exit 31. The entrance to the park is down a dirt road, and once inside the park, the road divides in two directions. The road to the battlefield and Redoubt #4 will take you past a beaver pond and creek (a picnic area overlooks part of the pond) where in spring can be found summer tanager, prothonotary warbler, northern parula warbler, yellow-throated warbler, great crested flycatcher, and a variety of other woodland species. In winter, sora and yellow rail can occassionally be heard at this pond. The road ends in an upland pine forest that has brown-headed nuthatch and pine warbler. Wild turkey may be seen in the field areas during winter.

The other branch of the road leads through the old town site and to the river. The old town site has many, large live oak trees, and northern parula warbler is abundant here in the spring. Along the river, a boardwalk trail takes you to views of the delta, distant views of the paper mills in northern Mobile, and through a cypress forest. Along the river, great crested flycatcher can often be seen in great abundance during spring. Also abundant during all the warmer months are insects, some with ferocious appetites; be prepared for bugs any time after March. Along the river, you may get views of swallow-tailed kite, tricolored heron, great blue heron, little blue heron, Caspian tern, barn swallow, yellow-throated warbler, pileated woodpecker, clapper rail, laughing gull, snowy egret, and other birds.

There are a number of other trails in the park that take you through the woods, along fields, along the embattlements, and to several ponds. In the woods, birds will be heard much more easily than they are seen. Camping is available. For more information, write or call Historic Blakeley Authority, 33707 St. Hwy 225, Spanish Fort, AL 36527, 205-626-0798.

## MEAHER STATE PARK

Meaher State Park provides a place to experience the marshland of the Mobile-Tensaw Rivers Delta where it meets Mobile Bay. Located on US 90/98, Meaher consists of about 1,300 acres of woods and swamp. The park is on the southern side of the highway between Mobile and Spanish Fort.

A trail through brush leads to a boardwalk that goes out over the water and through some of the marsh. Here can be seen swamp sparrow, seaside sparrow, and the secretive Henslow's sparrow in the reeds and brush of the marsh. At the edge of the marsh look for black-crowned night-heron and yellow-crowned night-heron, and, in winter, look for king rail and sora among the marsh grasses. Out in the water one can find brown pelican, royal and Caspian terns, numerous gull species, great blue heron, great egret, and snowy egret. While looking for birds in the marsh, scan the skies occasionally to look for high-flying peregrine falcons, particularly in winter and during migration seasons. A few falcons reside

*Peregrine Falcon*

in lower Alabama during the winter, and I have seen one from the boardwalk at Meaher State Park, but it was high up. Spring migrants will sometimes stop in the woods of the park and along the boardwalk, and yellow-rumped warblers winter here in healthy numbers.

# Chapter 2
# Lower Alabama

## CONECUH NATIONAL FOREST

 On the Alabama/Florida border, the Conecuh National Forest contains a number of southern coastal plain forest types, including pine woods, pine plantations, bottomland hardwood swamps, and some of the few remaining pitcher plant bogs. Most of the birds here are typical of coastal plain woodlands in the Deep South. Species of special interest include swallow-tailed kite along the waterways and fields and ground dove along fields and roadsides. The red-cockaded woodpecker does live on the national forest, and although seeing it is somewhat unlikely, there is two very accessible locations for attempting to spot this bird. The Conecuh can be hot, humid, insect-infested, and generally miserable during the summer months, but in winter, it provides a very pleasant area for hiking and camping. Spring migration will bring a number of species through the forests here, but seeing them is a chancy proposition. When hiking in winter, please check ahead of time for the hunting season schedule for the area; during certain hunting seasons, birding along the roads and near the campgrounds and ponds themselves would be safer than going through the woods. Bass fishing is sometimes pretty good in the ponds. During all times of the year, watch out for rattlesnakes, copperheads, and water moccasins. If you are careful where you step and where you place your hands, you should have no trouble from these snakes.

There are nice campgrounds at Blue Pond and Open Pond. *Warning:* Be careful when swimming in any waters in the Conecuh, as alligators are very numerous and have gotten as large as 12 feet long in recent years. They have attacked a few people in this area.

Driving along the forest roads will bring you through the various habitats in the national forest, but birding will be hit or miss. The areas to concentrate on include those around Blue and Open Ponds. The Conecuh Trail is a 20-mile-long trail that winds through the woods of the eastern part of the national forest. Having a number of loops in it, the trail provides the opportunity for outings of different lengths, long to short. The terrain is level and the hiking is very easy. The trail from Open Pond will give you the most variety of habitat in the shortest distance. The route the trail takes includes circumnavigating Open Pond itself, passing by three smaller ponds, climbing gently over a few foothills, passing by some swampy areas, and coming to the bank of Five Runs Creek and adjacent Blue Spring. Blue Spring is named for its most interesting blue shades of water. Cypress trees are widespread in these ponds and in the streams and rivers of the national forest.

Check the swampy, hardwood forests for warblers: orange-crowned and yellow-rumped in the winter, and prothonotary, Swainson's, common yellowthroat, hooded, and Louisiana waterthrush in the spring and summer. Solitary vireo can be readily seen in the woods near Open Pond during the winter. In woods with Spanish moss (such as near Alligator

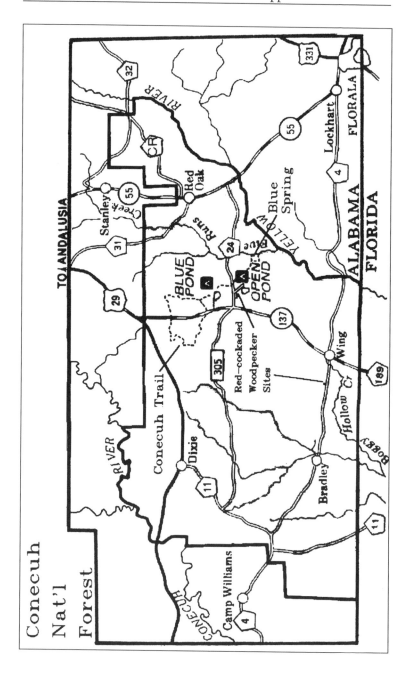

Hole, the smallest of the three ponds near Open Pond) listen and look for northern parula warbler.

The Conecuh Trail and the pond areas of the Conecuh National Forest can be reached by taking US 29 east from Brewton or west from Andalusia. Turn south on SH 137; after about 4 miles, the road to Blue Pond will be on the left; this is Forest Road 334. Another mile brings you to County Road 24; turn east, and in the short distance of 0.3 mile Forest Road 336 leads to the south; this road takes you to Open Pond and the southern portion of the trail.

There is a red-cockaded woodpecker viewing station just off CR 24 on the way to Open Pond. At the crest of the small hill between SH 137 and Forest Road 336 down to Open Pond is an unmarked dirt road to the south. Pull onto this dirt road and drive to a parking area with an information kiosk about the woodpecker. Visible from the sign are two nest cavity trees. The birds could be off foraging almost anywhere during the day, so your best chances of seeing them here are early in the morning, late in the afternoon, and during nesting season in the spring, when they will be returning regularly to feed their young.

As of late 1992, there was an active colony of red-cockaded woodpeckers right on the north side of County Road 4, west of the small town of Wing. Several active nesting trees are visible next to the road immediately west of where Forest Road 321 turns north from CR 4, approximately 1.5 miles west of Wing. There is plenty of room to park at the start of FR 321 and in a dirt patch just across the county road from FR 321. Down FR 321, there is a large pine tree at 0.95 mile; in late 1992 it appeared that woodpeckers were working on building nests in this tree. Since it takes red-cockaded woodpeckers several years to build a nesting hole, this tree bears watching in the future. At 1.1 miles from CR 4, FR 321 splits; take the right fork, FR 321A for 1.5 miles from County Road 4, and you will come to a gate. Approximately 100 feet off into the woods to the right is another nest tree for the woodpecker.

Other nest trees for the red-cockaded woodpecker can be seen from the various roads through the national forest, but none of those sites have as good a place to stop and observe as do the two spots described. Particular places to watch for the woodpeckers and their nesting trees are along County Road 4 east of where it hits County Road 11, about 7 miles west of the good site at FR 321, and along both sides of County Road 24 between the entrance to Open Pond and FR 337, two miles to the east.

For more information and a map of the Conecuh Trail, write to District Ranger's Office, Conecuh National Forest, P.O. Box 310, Andalusia, AL 36420; or write to Forest Supervisor, National Forests in Alabama, 2946 Chestnut Street, Montgomery, AL 36107.

## CHOCTAW NATIONAL WILDLIFE REFUGE

The Choctaw National Wildlife Refuge is located north of US 84 on the western bank of the Tombigbee River; it consists of over 4,200 acres of river, swamp, bottomland hardwood, and open field. The refuge protects the swamps where the Okatuppa and Turkey Creeks come into the Tombigbee. While not a very large refuge, Choctaw is heavily used by birds, and they make the most of almost every acre. Thousands of wood ducks nest there, and each winter there are hundreds of mallards and wigeons and lesser numbers of pintails, teal, ring-necked ducks, gadwalls, and northern shovelers. Spring brings nesting season for the wood ducks and for hundreds of herons, white ibis, egrets, and anhinga.

The refuge is reached by taking Choctaw County Road 21 north from US 84 near mile marker 14. County Road 21 dead-ends into County Road 14; turn east and drive 4.2 miles to Womack Hill, where a sign to the refuge will point down a dirt road to the south. This dirt road is rough and only one and a half lanes wide in places; but luckily, it soon turns to pavement. Just before this paved road reaches Lenoir Landing on the river, a dirt road to the west takes you a short distance to the entrance of the refuge. Signs prominently mark each turn.

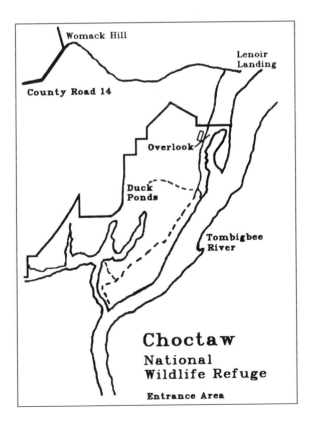

Being remote and lightly-visited, the refuge is not set up to handle large, or even moderate, numbers of visitors. This has worked out well for the birds, which get very little disturbance. Being closed from December 1 to March 1 each year, the refuge is mostly inaccessible during the prime wintering season for waterfowl. However, if you contact the refuge personnel prior to a visit during these dates, they will often make arrangements for you or your group to visit. Most of the refuge is inaccessible except by water; a boat ramp is provided near the entrance. During other times of the year, you can walk the roads of the refuge, or boat to the other parts of the refuge and walk through the woods. If you have access to a canoe, using it to glide through the hardwood swamps will give you not only a great birding experience but also a taste of the Deep South's wilder side. Summertime insects here can be voracious. White-tailed deer are extremely common in the woods and along the edges of the fields.

Just past the entrance is an information stand which overlooks a swampy portion of the river. In spring and summer, this area is a rookery for egrets, herons, ibises, and anhingas, and thus, this refuge provides one of the best viewing areas for anhinga in Alabama. The anhinga are most plentiful during the summer months but do occur on the refuge year-round, depending on weather conditions and other factors. Spring also brings swallow-tailed kites to the fields near the refuge entrance where they search for food in the newly mowed fields. Mississippi kites are also fairly common during the warmer months. Another rarity that frequents the refuge from spring through autumn is the wood stork. The species that nest in the swampy rookeries include white ibis, yellow-crowned night-heron, green-backed heron, little blue heron, snowy egret, great egret, and cattle egret.

*Anhinga*

Other birds of note that have been seen on the refuge include least bittern, American bittern, snow goose, purple gallinule, merlin, Cooper's hawk, and burrowing owl. Nesting songbirds in summer consist of prothonotary warbler, northern parula warbler, yellow-throated warbler, yellow-breasted chat, hooded warbler, American redstart, white-eyed vireo, red-eyed vireo, eastern bluebird, blue-gray gnatcatcher, yellow-billed cuckoo, wood thrush, and indigo bunting. Nesting raptors include red-shouldered hawk, red-tailed hawk, broad-winged hawk, and American kestrel.

*Green-backed Heron*

During the spring, when the dirt roads near the entrance are open, drive to the end of the main, more-traveled fork of the road alongside the river; it will dead-end where part of Okatuppa Creek comes into the Tombigbee. This is good viewing area over the river, and in the trees along the bank, prothonotary and parula warblers can be found at minimum focus range.

Bald eagles have been hacked on the refuge, and a number of them have begun to return. The hacking tower is in the field to the right of where the entrance road reaches the boat ramp.

Information and a partial bird list can be obtained from the Refuge Manager, Choctaw National Wildlife Refuge, P.O. Box 808, Jackson, AL 36545. This address gives you some idea of the remoteness of the refuge, as the headquarters is over

45 miles from the actual refuge itself. For information on arranging a possible winter visit to the closed portions of the refuge, call the headquarters at 205-246-3583.

## Blandon Springs State Park

Just a few miles south of Choctaw NWR is Blandon Springs State Park on Choctaw County Road 6, just northeast of the town of Blandon Springs on the eastern prong of CR 6. This is a 357-acre, day-use park that offers a very nice picnic area. The main park area consists of a series of small bathing pools with pumps to siphon the spring water; these are very relaxing on a warm day. Around the pools is a mixture of grass and pine woods with lots of edge habitat and hardwoods; in spring, birds are very abundant here. Listen and watch for yellow-throated warbler, northern parula warbler, great crested flycatcher, various woodpeckers, summer tanager, red-eyed vireo, pine warbler, American redstart, and Kentucky warbler.

The park is reached by taking either branch of County Road 6. The eastern branch goes south off SH 84 a couple of miles west of where it crosses the Tombigbee (CR 6 is sometimes not marked by a road sign here but there is usually a sign for the park) and is the most direct route. After 3.6 miles, you will see the dirt road entrance to the park on the right. Just a quarter mile past the park entrance is an intersection in the small town of Blandon Springs; the road to the north is the other branch of CR 6; to the south is County Road 31. This other, western branch of CR 6 intersects SH 84 just east of County Road 21, the way to the refuge.

## EUFAULA NATIONAL WILDLIFE REFUGE

The Eufaula National Wildlife Refuge is located along the Alabama-Georgia border at Lake Walter F. George. US 431 runs through part of the refuge and gives one easy access to this major wintering area for waterfowl. Comprised of over 11,000 acres, forty percent of which is water, Eufaula has sheltered as many as 40,000 ducks and 20,000 geese during the winter, but recent winters have seen a drastic decline in those numbers. During late winter and early spring, sandhill cranes have been spotted at Eufaula, mostly on the Georgia portion of the refuge. Bald eagles, wood storks, and peregrine falcons have also occasionally been seen.

The refuge is easily reached from US 431, north of the town of Eufaula. Take SH 165 east from US 431; turn right after 1.5 miles. This road is Old SH 165, and the entrance to the refuge is on the left after just a quarter mile. There are plenty of signs at all turns pointing the way to the refuge. Old SH 165 goes back south through Lake Point State Park to reconnect with US 431.

There is a woodland nature trail near the headquarters. A series of dirt roads (the Wing Spread Wildlife Drive) take you into a portion of the refuge and to an observation tower overlooking part of the impounded waters. Sighting ducks and geese from areas along the water is hit-or-miss during years when the numbers of wintering waterfowl are low. Rusty blackbirds can be found in the woods near the observation tower during the winter. The fields along the roads are a good place to see red-tailed hawk, northern harrier, American kestrel, eastern meadowlark, vesper sparrows, water pipit, turkey vulture, black vulture, field sparrow, and eastern bluebird.

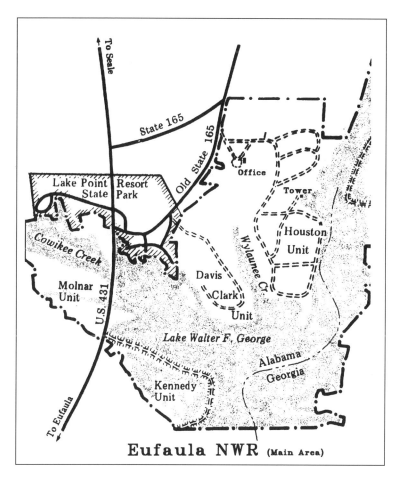

Eufaula NWR (Main Area)

The Kennedy Impoundment unit is located south of the bridge over the lake, south of Lakepoint State Park; there is a dirt access road off to the east of US 431. Park here and walk along the dike to get views of ponds, fields, and the lake. Various egrets, great blue heron, kingfisher, and waterfowl can be seen in this area. Around the parking area in spring and summer, check the Spanish-moss-draped oak trees for northern parula warbler.

A map, information, and a bird list containing 281 species can be acquired by writing Refuge Manager, Eufaula National Wildlife Refuge, Route 2, Box 97-B, Eufaula, AL 36027-9294.

### Lakepoint Resort State Park

Located in the middle of the wildlife refuge and right on US 431 is the heavily developed Lakepoint Resort State Park. This park is mostly a marina, a lodge, and a large parking lot with a small beach. However, Canada geese often congregate here in the winter; sometimes, as many as a hundred or more wander around the parking lot, the beach, and the grassy area in between. Mallards collect near the lodge, which can be seen from the beach. Many of these ducks and geese have become domesticated and depend on handouts from the lodge. Many gulls, mostly ring-billed, gather here. Both American crow and fish crow occur here, and this park gives you a good opportunity to practice distinguishing between them. Information on lodging at the park can be obtained by calling 800-544-LAKE, or writing to Lakepoint Resort State Park, P.O. Box 267, Eufaula, AL 36072-0267.

### TUSKEGEE NATIONAL FOREST

East of Montgomery, near Auburn and Tuskegee, is one of the nation's smallest national forests, in terms of size. However, the Tuskegee National Forest has a subtle beauty, and being right next to I-85, it is extremely accessible. At exit 42, take SH 186 south from I-85, and you will reach the forest in about a mile; the ranger station is but 1.8 miles from the interstate, on the left. Just past the ranger station is the

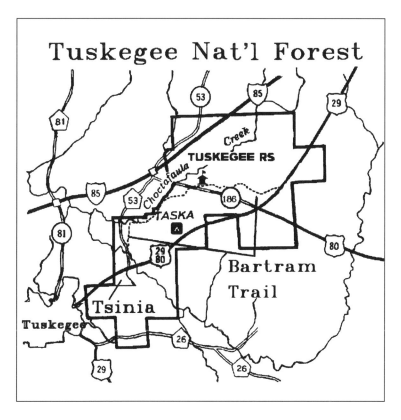

Atasi picnic ground and parking area that gives you access
to the Bartram Trail. Named for the naturalist William Bartram, the trail is 8.5 miles long and runs the length of the
national forest. This parking area hits the trail just about at
its midpoint, and hiking trips of almost any length can be easily planned for the Bartram Trail. The eastern end of the trail
is on US 29, about a mile east of its intersection with US 80,
and the western terminus of the trail is at a parking area on
County Road 53, about a mile north of where CR 53 meets
US 80. With only gentle hills in this area, the trail is an easy
walk for almost everyone.

Winding through various habitats such as upland pine forest, bottomland hardwoods, and streamside forest and swamp, the trail offers a variety of birding opportunities. Just west of the parking area near the ranger station, a fairly open pine forest is a good spot to look for abundant pine warbler, brown-headed nuthatch, white-breasted nuthatch, wild turkey, red-headed woodpecker, eastern bluebird, red-bellied woodpecker, and great crested flycatcher. Prairie warblers can be found in the summer in low, young pines that make up some of the replanted clearcut areas in the forest. East of the parking lot at the ranger station, in ravine areas where hardwoods dominate, solitary vireos can be found in winter. The more mature pine stands in the forest have mostly been cut down and replaced with short-term rotation pine plantations; therefore, most of this area that was once suitable for supporting the red-cockaded woodpecker is no longer, as the bird requires pine trees over 60 years of age and prefers trees over 100 years old. The status of the species is very weak in this area. There is probably not enough good habitat to sustain a viable population now; nonetheless, I saw one in this area many years ago. So, when in any areas of large pines, keep a lookout for this endangered bird, and with a great deal of luck, you might see one. The trail itself goes through a number of pine areas, which alternate with cutover areas, swamps, and bottom hardwoods; some large, old pine trees do remain.

In some of these hardwood and swampy areas, particularly on the trail west of SH 186, nesting warblers can be found in spring and early summer. Look for prothonotary warbler, hooded warbler, American redstart, yellow-throated warbler, and Louisiana waterthrush. There are a number of short, side trails that lead down to Choctafaula Creek, which is a pleasant stream that winds between sandy banks that make good picnic spots. Along these stream banks and the surrounding woods, watch for yellow warbler.

At the far western end of the national forest, on US 80, just before it goes into the town of Tuskegee, is the Tsinia Wildlife Viewing Area. The parking lot for Tsinia is on Forest Road 937, just south of that road's juncture with US 80. This area has been designed with trails, fields, and an observation blind in the middle of a lake, and it is an easily accessible place for watching birds. The lake will have ducks such as mallards in the winter and wood ducks year-round. Watch for belted kingfishers and eastern phoebes. With a great deal of edge habitat, Tsinia is a good spot for birds such as migrating warblers; in winter, ruby-crowned kinglet is common, and orange-crowned warbler, hermit thrush, winter wren, and house wren can be sighted. In summer, there are prairie warblers. I have regularly seen a red-shouldered hawk patrolling the sky over Tsinia.

While in the area, spend some time in Tuskegee, for it is a very historic town. Here is the home of Tuskegee Institute, founded by Booker T. Washington, and it is one of the premier African-American universities in the country.

For information, a map of the national forest, and a map of the Bartram Trail, write to: U.S. Forest Service, Route 1, Box 457, Tuskegee, AL 36083, or Forest Supervisor, National Forests in Alabama, 2946 Chestnut Street, Montgomery, AL 36107.

## MONTGOMERY

The capital of Alabama, Montgomery is centrally located in the state. Although it offers some fair birding to local residents who have the time to become intimately familiar with the town, Montgomery does not provide much birding for the traveler or short-term visitor. Lagoon Park on the northeastern portion of the city's bypass does offer the largest amount of open land that is readily accessible to the public. This park has a great deal of space devoted to softball parks, tennis courts, and a golf course, but there is still plenty of land left in woodlands, ponds, and open fields. The northern part of Lagoon Park is more productive for birding, providing hardwoods, pine forests, fields, and marshy, pondside areas. Here can be found great blue heron, eastern meadowlark, eastern phoebe, kingfisher, American kestrel, various woodpeckers, field sparrow, killdeer, pine warbler, and loggerhead shrike. In winter, white-throated sparrow, song sparrow, northern junco, and orange-crowned warbler live in Lagoon Park. Also, during winter, look for common snipe in the reeds and marshy areas along the pond edges. It is the only place inside a large town or city where I have readily seen eastern bluebirds.

To get to the northern part of the park, either go behind the park from the entrance on the bypass, Eastern Boulevard (US 231), or follow the signs to the Pete Peterson Lodge from the first intersection south of the bypass on Congressman Dickinson Drive. Watch the open fields for birds, but walk along the brushy edges of the woods for the most productive birding.

Other than birding, Montgomery does provide visitors with a number of interesting things to do. Of particular note are the beautiful Alabama Shakespeare Festival and Montgomery Museum, which share the same park on the eastern bypass. These two facilities and many smaller art and theater organizations contribute to a cultural richness in Montgomery that is often not found in cities many times its size. At the very least, when passing through Montgomery, one will

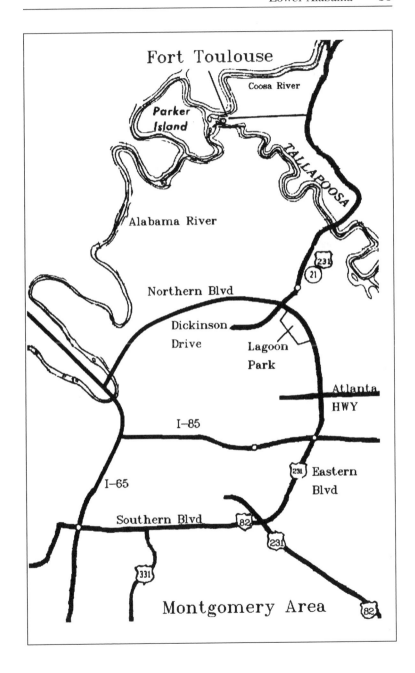

Fort Toulouse

Coosa River

Parker Island

TALLAPOOSA

Alabama River

Northern Blvd

Dickinson Drive

Lagoon Park

Atlanta HWY

I-85

231
21

I-65

231 Eastern Blvd

Southern Blvd

82

231

331

Montgomery Area

82

want to see a play at the Shakespeare Festival, if it is in season. For information on the play schedule, call 205-277-
BARD. The Shakespeare Festival has a large pond in front
of it that was designed for domesticated swans; a few years
ago, a flock of migrating Canada geese saw the pond, stopped,
and never left. Although these geese were a great attraction
for many Montgomerians, the developer who built the Festival disliked them because "his" pond had been designed with
only swans in mind. So, in early 1992, the geese were drugged,
removed, sent to private ponds and had their wings clipped
so that they could not return. This incident illustrates the lack
of sensitivity wild birds often face and how people often do
not consider wild birds proper parts of their environment.

## FORT TOULOUSE

Located on the peninsula where the Coosa and Tallapoosa
Rivers come together to form the Alabama River, Fort
Toulouse is a historic park that preserves re-creations of
two forts that were built on the site during the early 1800s.
The park is owned by the State of Alabama and is bordered,
in parts, by land owned by the United States Army Corps of
Engineers. To get to Fort Toulouse, turn west onto Ft.
Toulouse Road off US 231, south of Wetumpka; a shop-
ping center called Bienville Square with a Big B drugstore
and a Food World is just across the highway from Ft.
Toulouse Road, and a Wal-Mart is just to the south from the
turn. A short drive of approximately three miles through pas-
tureland and marshy woods will bring you to the entrance
to Fort Toulouse; keep a lookout for red-tailed hawks and
American kestrels along the road, particularly in winter.
The park is open during daylight hours. There is a $1

entrance fee for adults, 50 cents for children, and camping is available from April through October.

At the western end of the parking lot, there begins the William Bartram Arboretum nature trail, which will take you through the hardwood forest and the swamp to the Tallapoosa River. Also at the end of the parking lot is a dirt road which is the path that leads through a field to the reconstructed Fort Toulouse. The park provides several major habitats for birds: hardwood swamp, upland hardwoods, and open field. Because of the small size of the park, all three areas can be extensively explored within a few hours.

The Bartram nature trail is a boardwalk that goes through the upland hardwoods and then descends to the swampier woods below. It is named in honor of the naturalist William Bartram who traveled through Alabama in 1775–1776 and passed very close to the confluence of the Coosa and Tallapoosa Rivers; possibly, he walked through these same woods. Along the upper part of the trail, every species of woodpecker found in Alabama, except for the red-cockaded, can be spotted. Frequently sighted in the summer are great crested flycatcher and northern parula warbler which feed and nest among the Spanish moss in the larger trees. Carolina chickadee, Carolina wren, and tufted titmouse are ubiquitous. Where a bridge on the trail spans a small ravine, look for hermit thrush in winter and wood thrush in summer. In winter, the woods also provide occasionally large flocks of yellow-rumped warblers, white-throated sparrows, and rusty blackbirds. Further down in the bottoms along the river, prothonotary warbler and hooded warbler can be found nesting during the summer. During winter, this trail can lead to such birds as hermit thrush, winter wren, house wren, and even Bewick's wren, which is quite scarce in Alabama. Rufous-sided towhee is seen regularly, thrashing about in the leaves on the forest floor; brown thrashers are almost always seen.

In the woods along the edges of the fields, look for the secretive Lincoln's sparrow in winter. Winter also brings in large numbers of white-throated sparrows and occasionally fox sparrows to the fields of Fort Toulouse. Flocks of eastern meadowlarks are common. Belted kingfishers can be seen flying over the fields from one river to the other and in the trees along the banks. I have been lucky enough to see male and female bobolinks in a field at Toulouse as they stopped to rest on their spring migration to the northern United States. There is an Indian mound west of the reconstructed Fort Toulouse, and the woods on top of it often contain a number of birds; this mound is of the Mississippian phase, circa 1100–1400 A.D. In the woods on the mound and the woods between it and the fort, watch for woodpeckers and, in winter, groups of ruby-crowned and golden-crowned kinglets and northern juncos. The park has a bluebird trail of nest boxes along the roads and the edges of the fields, and eastern bluebirds can often be seen. Also watch for loggerhead shrike along the edges of the woods.

# Chapter 3
# Mountains and Piedmont

## MOUND STATE MONUMENT

 In the town of Moundville, a truly fascinating collection of earthen mounds and other artifacts of a large Southeastern Indian city are preserved in Mound State Monument. The monument is located right on the Black Warrior River, and over its 317 acres is much open field and edge habitat for birds. Grassland species such as eastern meadowlark and eastern bluebird, and wintering sparrows such as white-throated, fox, vesper, song, and savannah sparrows can be sighted; wintering red-tailed hawks, American kestrels, and northern harrier are also possible. In winter, the river can yield various ducks, gulls, and occasional common loons. Summer brings a number of songbirds such as indigo bunting, summer tanager, blue grosbeak, dickcissel, and a variety of woodland and swamp warblers including prothonotary, northern parula, yellow-throated, black-and-white, American redstart, hooded, and Kentucky. Although I know of no unusual species that regularly occur at Moundville, the combination of woodland, field, and river habitats in close proximity make for good birding.

The impressive mounds and the displays of artifacts make Moundville a worthwhile stop if one is in the area and has any interest in the history of the native inhabitants of the South. A one-way drive winds through the fields and the mounds (there are 20 of them still intact) and leads down to the river. The park is located just west of SH 69, on the northern end of town; there are signs that guide you right to the park. Moundville is about 13 miles south of Tuscaloosa. More information on the park and on the history of the Native Americans who lived there can be obtained from Alabama State Museum of Natural History, Mound State Monument, P.O. Box 66, Moundville, AL 35474.

## CAHABA RIVER

One of the last free-flowing rivers in Alabama, the Cahaba is the most biologically diverse river of its size in the entire nation. Crossing a number of different geologic provinces as it flows from northeast of Birmingham down to the Alabama River west of Selma, the Cahaba is the home of over 130 species of fish, including several species that live only there. The Cahaba has numerous species of rare, endangered mussels and has several aquatic insect species that are found nowhere else. Also found in the Cahaba is the rare Cahaba lily, which lives in the rocky shoals in the middle of the riverbed and puts on unimaginably beautiful displays of flowers for three to four weeks during late May and early June. Although there is some good birding along the river, the lilies are the real show.

Most of the river flows through private land, and unless one takes a canoe trip down the river, there is very little public access to this beautiful and ecologically significant waterway. However, the land along the western bank of the river opposite the major shoals of lily habitat is owned by a paper company that allows public access to about two miles of the river. Here, in Bibb County, one can get in some good birding while seeing the rare and spectacular sight of thousands of Cahaba lilies blooming in the middle of the river. The combination of spring songbirds and the blooming of the lilies really makes late May the best time to bird here. With some luck, other times of the year can be productive for birding, and the river is certainly good for canoeing and sightseeing at all times when the water is high enough. The Cahaba is considered by many to be the finest canoe ride in the state; there are no large rapids, and there is a variety of habitats to choose from to canoe through.

Take SH 25 west from I-65 at the Calera/Montevallo exit (exit 228); SH 25 goes through Calera by turning south and then west again. Past Montevallo and the small town of Wilton, watch for Bibb County Road 65 on the right. Take County Road 65 to where it dead-ends in a T intersection, and turn left (west); although it is sometimes unmarked by signs, County Road 65 continues to the west. Two miles past this intersection, you will reach Piper Bridge over the Cahaba; continue 0.3 miles, and turn onto a dirt road on the left. This is a well-graded road that goes back down to the river; a good parking area is available right where the road meets the river and turns right. The small stream next to the parking area is called the Little Ugly. The dirt road continues on downstream along the bank of the river for a couple of miles, but it can be rutted and washed out at times; it is best to park at the river and walk the road to the shoals areas.

After 0.25 mile, you will reach the first shoals, and the stand of lilies here can be very beautiful. Watch for Louisiana waterthrush wading among the lilies and feeding along the large puddles in the road. Watch for various

*Louisiana Waterthrush*

swallows feeding over the water, particularly near dusk. Yellow-throated warbler, northern parula warbler, and acadian flycatcher are spring and summer residents in the woods here. Great blue heron is common in the river, and wood ducks can be seen flying over the river. The woods contain the usual woodland species here, and pileated woodpeckers are fairly abundant.

Another mile down the road, after wading across a small stream, you come to Hargrove Shoals, which contains the largest stand of Cahaba lilies in the world. When in full bloom, the lilies here provide a natural wonder to rival any on Earth. Bring a pair of old tennis shoes and a walking stick for balance, and walk out into the water among the lilies. Under normal spring conditions, the water is shallow (rarely more than two feet deep), and you can walk among the flowers and smell their perfume in the air. Be careful, some of the rocks are slippery. Flyfishing for bass, including the Alabama spotted bass, is very good here.

The Cahaba is an extremely beautiful and biologically significant river, but it is in serious danger. Pollution from Birmingham area sewers, industrial discharges, agricultural chemicals, development runoff, and siltation are literally killing the river and its unique lifeforms. The amount of the river that can sustain life is reduced each year; yet, the state and federal governments adamantly refuse to do anything to protect the Cahaba; too many large businesses and government bodies in the Birmingham area depend upon polluting the Cahaba in order to make money. Further, virtually none of the land along the banks of the river is protected. However, there are people working to protect this special river. For more information about the Cahaba or for information on canoe trips being run throughout the year, contact The Cahaba River Society, 2717 7th Avenue, South, Suite 205, Birmingham, AL 35233.

## TALLADEGA NATIONAL FOREST

Talladega National Forest is the largest in Alabama and is divided into two widely separated parts. The Oakmulgee Ranger District is located south of Tuscaloosa and west of I-65; the Shoal Creek and Talladega Ranger Districts are located together east of I-65 in the highest mountains in the state. This national forest offers some of the best camping, hiking, and backpacking opportunities in Alabama, and the birding on this forest can occasionally be very good.

### Oakmulgee Ranger District

This portion of the Talladega National Forest is undoubtedly one of the most important areas for the endangered

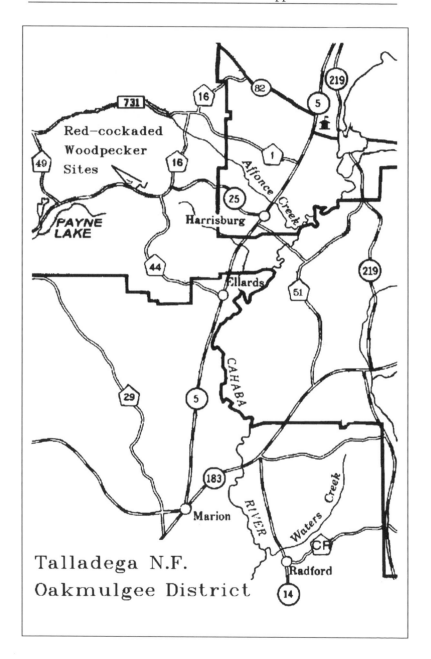

red-cockaded woodpecker, as this ranger district has more woodpecker colonies than any other area in Alabama and Mississippi. As of early 1992, Oakmulgee had more than 300 colonies with over 130 of them being active at the time. The map of the forest at the district ranger station in Centerville is virtually covered with the outlines of the colonies and the dots that indicate the trees used for nesting. The number of woodpeckers here is so high (relative to their scarcity elsewhere) that many of these colony trees are right next to roadways, including some next to a state highway that runs through the forest. This ease of access to the colony trees means that the visiting birder has an excellent opportunity for watching red-cockaded woodpeckers in a large, remaining portion of their natural habitat. With so many of the protected birds, not nearly as much of Oakmulgee has fallen prey to the clearcuts and the short-term rotation of pine plantations that have taken over many of our national forests. Thus, large expanses of natural, old-age pine forests can be found, and these beautiful forests provide a chance to see the South as much of it once was.

The easiest spot to locate red-cockaded woodpeckers on the Oakmulgee is just off SH 25. Take SH 5 south from Brent about 5 miles until SH 25 forks to the west. Travel along SH 25 approximately 6 miles and watch for the road to the Pondville lookout tower on the right. About a mile past the road to the tower, Forest Road 753 will be on the right; this is a gated road, but there is plenty of space to park at the entrance to this road. Walk down this road through an old clearcut until you reach mature pine forest in less than 0.5 mile; this stand of forest on top of several pretty hills holds a number of nesting trees for the woodpecker. These trees are marked with twelve-inch bands of blue paint. This colony covers a fairly large area, and by listening carefully for the bird, one should be able to find the woodpecker at almost any time of day and year. Dawn and spring nesting season increase one's chances of seeing the woodpeckers. Also in these woods, particularly in the spring, look for pine warbler, prairie warbler (particularly in the clearcut), yellow-throated warbler, summer tanager, indigo bunting, eastern peewee, and a variety of sparrows.

If this area is unproductive for the woodpecker, go just 0.2 mile further down SH 25; on the right (northern side) will be a jeep track leading up a hill into some obviously managed pines. Wherever there are woodpeckers in the Oakmulgee, the Forest Service cuts out the hardwood understory and actively manages the sites for the woodpeckers' benefit. Areas so managed are easily spotted when driving along the roads of this forest, as these areas have many large pines within an open, grassy expanse. There are a number of nesting trees in the woods on this hillside, and you can follow the jeep track up the hill through the center of these pines. Watch for palm warblers during the winter and early Spring.

The Oakmulgee ranger station is located on the east side of SH 5, just south of where it intersects with US 82, north of Brent. Information about the forest and about other places to try to find red-cockaded woodpeckers can be obtained here, but only on weekdays; the station is closed on the weekends. The many forest roads are dirt, but the vast majority of them are well maintained and passable to any car. Describing the sites of all the red-cockaded woodpecker colonies on the Oakmulgee is well beyond the scope of this book, but the folks at the ranger station can show you where they all are, if you are interested in seeing them. A number of environmental groups in Alabama are trying to get Congress to designate part of the Oakmulgee as a wilderness area in order to give the woodpeckers even more legal protection.

Other than the opportunity to see red-cockaded woodpeckers in perhaps their last major stronghold, Oakmulgee offers the species normally seen in the central Alabama woodlands and foothills. Pine warblers and brown-headed nuthatches are quite abundant, as are the more common varieties of woodpeckers.

## Talladega and Shoal Creek Ranger Districts

Located east of Birmingham in the highest range of mountains in Alabama, these two combined ranger districts provide excellent hiking, camping, and backpacking opportunities. Once home to a fair number of red-cockaded woodpeckers, this portion of the Talladega is now nothing like the Oakmulgee Division; the number of active colonies here is down to virtually none. Short-term rotation of the pine timber base has resulted in a forest that simply is not old enough to provide for these woodpeckers.

Scenically speaking, this area of Alabama is perhaps its most beautiful, as trails and scenic highways run along high mountain ridges that overlook valleys as much as 1,200 feet below. Cheaha State Park is located in the middle of this portion of Talladega National Forest; it contains the state's highest point and is discussed in its own section. The high mountains here do allow for the summer presence of birds that are normally found only in more northerly areas. Sharp-shinned hawks and black-throated green warblers have been known to nest in the high areas of the forest's ridges.

The most visited part of the forest is the Cheaha Wilderness, immediately south of Cheaha State Park. This is

*Sharp-shinned Hawk*

Alabama's second largest (out of only two) wilderness area, with approximately 7,800 acres, and it preserves the highest peaks of the Talladega National Forest. A well developed set of trails crosses the Cheaha Wilderness from one side to the other and allows birders access to wooded ridges and scenic overlooks. The birds here are typical of the rugged hardwood forests of this area. There were once a few active red-cockaded woodpecker colonies at the very western portion of the wilderness area, but to see one of these birds there now would be extraordinarily lucky. The Odum Scout Trail runs for ten miles through the wilderness in a south-north direction, and the northern half of the trail is part of the 100-mile-long Pinhoti Trail. The southern terminus of the Odum Trail is near Pyriton; to reach it, follow the signs west from SH 49, north of Lineville. This part of the trail climbs a small, scenic ravine with a pretty waterfall (when there is sufficient water) and then follows a ridge to a beautiful overlook of the wilderness about two miles from the trailhead. The northern portion of Odum Trail is more accessible as the trailhead is in Cheaha State Park, right on the Talladega Scenic Drive as it enters the park from the east.

The Chinnabee Silent Trail, built by scouts from a deaf troop, connects the Pinhoti and Odum Trails in the Cheaha Wilderness with Lake Chinnabee, six miles west of where the trails meet. This trail provides access to lower forests where birds such as white-breasted nuthatch, pine warbler, brownheaded nuthatch, yellow-shafted flicker, and eastern bluebird are quite common year-round. Much of this trail follows Cheaha Creek, which is very pretty and which has a beautiful set of waterfalls on it. Lake Chinnabee is a good camping spot; it is reached by taking Forest Road 646 south off CR 42, two miles west of Cheaha State Park. CR 42 provides the only direct access to the park from the western side.

The Pinhoti Trail is Alabama's longest trail, and it is still in development. Recent acquisitions to Talladega National Forest will make it possible to extend the trail all the way to the Georgia border. There are long-range plans to some day connect the Pinhoti to the Appalachian Trail. This trail

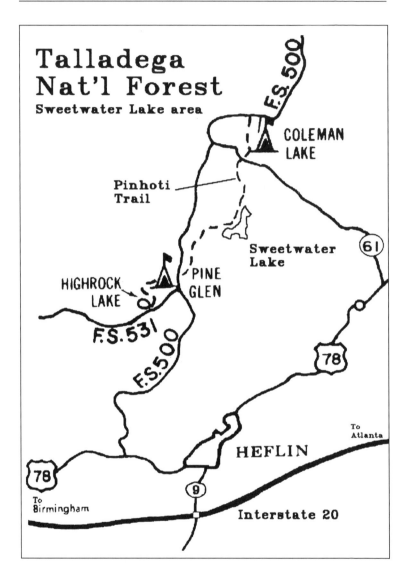

# Talladega Nat'l Forest

**Sweetwater Lake area**

F.S. 500

COLEMAN LAKE

Pinhoti Trail

Sweetwater Lake

61

HIGHROCK LAKE

PINE GLEN

F.S. 531

F.S. 500

78

HEFLIN

To Atlanta

78

9

To Birmingham

Interstate 20

runs most of the length of this portion of the national forest, in a generally north-south direction. Dugger Mountain, at the northern end of the trail, is being considered as a possible wilderness area, but access to that area is currently limited to foot travel. The portions of the Pinhoti Trail through the Cheaha Wilderness and Cheaha State Park and through the Sweetwater Lake area are the most accessible. These areas of the trail also give birders best access to the woods, away from the roads. For backpackers, this trail is the best in this two-state area.

The Sweetwater Lake area consists of three lakes in the portion of the forest north of I-20 and Heflin. Coleman Lake provides an excellent camping area, and the Pinhoti Trail connects that lake with Sweetwater Lake and Highrock Lake. These lakes and the surrounding woods provide good spring and summer bird habitat for belted kingfisher, broad-winged hawk, yellow-throated warbler, black-and-white warbler, pine warbler, worm-eating warbler, and brown-headed nuthatch. Check clearcuts and other recently logged areas along the forest roads for prairie warblers. To reach Coleman Lake and the campground, take Forest Road 553 northwest from US 78, north of Heflin; when FR 553 hits FR 500, follow FR 500 to the right and to the lake (there are signs). I have found that broad-winged hawks around Coleman Lake are very easy to call up with a good hawk call. Also, early evenings in the spring and summer provide a good display of bats over the lake as they drink and eat insects.

## CHEAHA STATE PARK

Containing Alabama's highest point, 2,407-foot Mt. Cheaha, Cheaha State Park is home to a number of hawk species, and it provides the southernmost known nesting area of the black-throated green warbler. The park has a modern lodge and restaurant, campgrounds, a small recreational lake, and a number of cabins and chalets. Many short trails lead to beau-

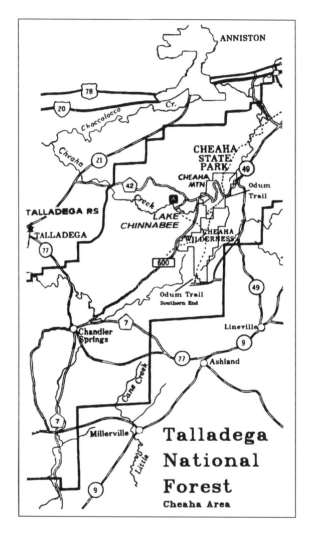

tiful cliffs overlooking the valley 1,200 feet below and give views into the Cheaha Wilderness area to the south in Talladega National Forest. Indeed, the entire 2,700-acre state park is surrounded by the national forest, and an extensive drive through the forest is required to get to the park.

To reach Cheaha State Park from the west, turn east from SH 21 onto Talladega County Road 96, which is paved, and CR 96 will take you to County Road 42; there are signs on SH 21 and CR 96 indicating where to turn. Follow this winding road until you reach the park; watch out for log trucks. From the northeast, take US 431 south from its intersection with I-20; about 4 miles later, turn right onto SH 49, the Talladega Scenic Drive, which will take you directly into the park. From the southeast, take SH 49 north out of Lineville from its intersection with SH 9; this portion of SH 49, which is not part of the designated scenic drive will dead-end into the scenic drive; turn left and go on into the park.

Hawks that nest on or near Mt. Cheaha include red-shouldered, red-tailed, broad-winged, and sharp-shinned; they can often be seen with their fledglings during late spring and early summer. During spring and fall migration one can sometimes see many hawks flying past the cliffs of the park, but as with many birding activities, it is a hit-or-miss thing. I have been there some days and seen dozens of hawks within a few hours and on other days seen none at all. There is always the possibility of a Cooper's hawk passing by the cliffs.

Other spring and summer birds of note at Cheaha are the black-throated green warbler, worm-eating warbler, indigo bunting, summer tanager, scarlet tanager, and ovenbird. I have never had much luck with fall migrants here; however, the autumn colors of the changing leaves can be very spectacular at the park. Sitting at the cliff just below the restaurant in summer and early fall can provide nice views of bats silhouetted against the colors of the sunset as they leave their roosts in the trees and cliffs below.

Part of the 100-mile-long Pinhoti Trail runs through Cheaha State Park. That trail is discussed in the section on the Talladega National Forest.

More information, and details about camping, rooms at the lodge, or renting a cabin or chalet can be obtained by writing: Division of State Parks, Alabama Dept. of Conservation and Natural Resources, 64 North Union Street, Montgomery, AL 36130. Or you can call 1-800-ALA-PARK, nationwide.

## OAK MOUNTAIN STATE PARK

As the state's largest state park, just south of Birmingham, Alabama's largest city, Oak Mountain State Park gets a great deal of use. Thus, much of the park has been extensively developed for modern recreation, and this development includes large man-made lakes, a golf course, a demonstration farm, riding stables, tennis courts, cottages, a big campground, and much more. The park's almost 10,000 acres also include room for 31.5 miles of trails through its wilder, undeveloped portions. This extensive trail system allows for day hikes or backpacking trips of almost any length. Most of the trails provide access to the various pine, hardwood, and mixed forests that cover Double Oak Mountain and its surrounding foothills.

Although it can get hot in the summer, Oak Mountain State Park is a good location for year-round birding. Winter is good for extensive hiking with comfortable temperatures and no hunting to worry about. Because it is a protected area of significant size in the midst of urban and suburban development and agricultural areas, Oak Mountain attracts a fair number of migrant species during the spring and autumn. Catching species of birds that do not nest in Alabama but only migrate through to the north is largely a matter of luck, but Oak Mountain provides an easily accessible place to spot migrants in the middle of the state.

In autumn, the campground is a good spot to look for migrants. Large flocks of mixed warblers such as black-throated green warbler, common yellowthroat, ruby-crowned kinglet, golden-crowned kinglet, and other warblers in their

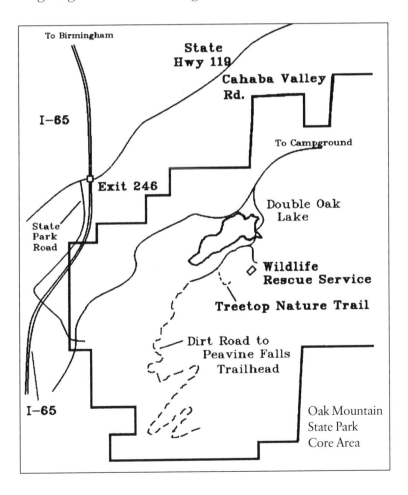

drabber plumage pass through. Woodpeckers are also easy to spot in the campground, along with standard birds such as white-breasted nuthatch, Carolina chickadee, tufted titmouse, Carolina wren, and field sparrow. On some of the trails through the foothills near the campground, keep a look out for migrating Swainson's thrush during the fall; I have spotted them several times along the Shakleford Point trail in the hollow near to where that trail hits the Foothills trail at the main road.

An extensive bluebird trail in the park provides a healthy population of eastern bluebirds. Look for them along the road, in the golf course, and alongside the parking lot at the Alabama Wildlife Rescue Service center. The private AWRS is headquartered in the old restaurant in the park; follow the signs from the recreation lake. At the AWRS, thousands of injured and orphaned animals and birds are cared for each year; the goal of the group is to rehabilitate these creatures

*Eastern Bluebird*

so that they can be released back into the wild. The care of injured wild animals and birds is fascinating to learn about, and this facility allows visitors to see what is being done and to watch some of the animals and birds from behind one-way glass. An excellent learning opportunity for children and adults alike, the AWRS center is a must-see place while at Oak Mountain.

Also stop by the Treetop Nature Trail across from the park headquarters. Operated by the AWRS, this boardwalk trail takes you up into the trees and has a number of large, elevated cages enclosing birds of prey that have been too severely injured to be released back into the wild. Usually on display are barred owl, great horned owl, red-shouldered hawk, red-tailed hawk, and black vulture. The trail also has a rare, albino barred owl. In spring, many migrating songbirds can be seen from the Treetop Nature Trail and from the ground-level trails that lead into the woods from the nature trail.

The dirt road that goes to Peavine Falls takes you up to the top of Oak Mountain and provides good views over the valley below. Stopping at one of the picnic tables or other clear areas here will give you the best chance of spotting soaring raptors. With a variety of woodland and field habitats, Oak Mountain State Park provides for a variety of birds of prey. Wintering raptors include northern harrier and merlin. American kestrel, red-tailed hawk, red-shouldered hawk, turkey vulture, and black vulture are year-round residents. Summer finds broad-winged hawks in the park, and both migration seasons mean that any of those species plus Cooper's hawk and sharp-shinned hawk could pass by on the wind currents along the mountain side. At night, the woods of Oak Mountain State Park are sometimes filled with the calls of barred owl, great horned owl, and eastern screech owl, all year-round residents.

To reach Oak Mountain State Park, take exit 246 (Cahaba Valley Road) off I-65; go west and take the first road to the south that is west of the interstate; there are signs. This road is State Park Road, and it will go south, then east under the interstate. When it comes to a four-way intersection, turn left, and you will go straight into the park. There is a $1 per person entrance fee. There is a back way into the park found by going east on north SH 119; this back entrance to Oak Mountain State Park is located on SH 119, 5.7 miles from the interstate, and the signs say "Oak Mountain Lake" but do not mention the park. A short drive over a ridge on this road will take you into the park. After driving over a dam for one of the park's lakes, this road will wind through the park and connect with the road coming in from the main entrance.

More information, a map of the trails, and details about camping or renting a cottage can be obtained by writing: Division of State Parks, Alabama Dept. of Conservation and Natural Resources, 64 North Union Street, Montgomery, AL 36130. Or you can call 1-800-ALA-PARK, nationwide.

## BIRMINGHAM

Alabama's largest city started out as an industrial center where steel and iron were the mainstays of the economy. Heavy industry still plays a big part in Birmingham, but the city has broadened to become a commercial and banking center as well. Having grown to its current size, Birmingham has lost most of its original wild bird habitat. Nonetheless, migrants still stop here, particularly in the wooded suburbs on the south side of the city. Describing where to bird in most of Birmingham would be difficult, but a call to the Alabama Ornithological Society's Rare Bird Hotline, 205-987-2730, is

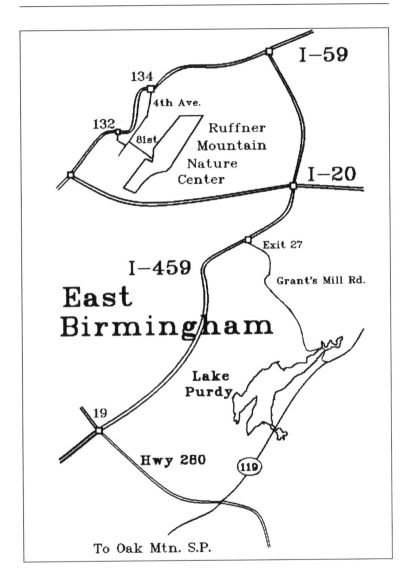

worthwhile before any trip to the Birmingham area, because rare accidentals are often sighted in Birmingham. Perhaps it is just the greater number of birders there. For example, the only varied thrush seen in Alabama was found in a yard in one of the wealthier bedroom communities south of town in early 1992.

One spot worth visiting while in Birmingham is the Ruffner Mountain Nature Center. This 538-acre preserve right in town allows one to see some of the unique geology of the area, and it contains some remnant woodland on one of the ridges in the eastern part of the city. Twenty-six warbler species, inhabitants and migrants, have been sighted at Ruffner Mountain; some of the rarer ones for this area are the Cape May Warbler and the chestnut-sided warbler. Otherwise, any of the woodland species that inhabit Alabama may be seen at Ruffner.

To reach the Nature Center, take exit 133 off I-59 coming from downtown Birmingham, north of where I-59 diverges from I-20; go south (right) on 4th Avenue South, and then turn left on 81st Street South and follow it to the Center. Coming into town on I-59, take exit 132 (northbound and southbound exits are numbered separately); turn left on SH 11 (1st Avenue North), go under the interstate and immediately turn left onto 80th Street at the first traffic light. Then go to 4th Avenue South, turn left and then turn right after one block onto 81st Street. 81st Street South will dead-end into the refuge; there is a Dead End sign with a Ruffner Mountain sign below it. The headquarters is an old house on the right. Continuing past the gate a short ways will take you to a parking lot, a gift shop, and the trailhead for the park's seven miles of trails. The park is open Tuesday through Saturday, 9:00 a.m. to 5:00 p.m., and Sunday, 1:00 p.m. to 5:00 p.m.; it is closed on Mondays. For more information on the preserve, write Ruffner Mountain Nature Center, 1214 81st Street South, Birmingham, AL 35206.

## Lake Purdy

Just south of the city is Lake Purdy, which is owned by the Birmingham Water and Sewer Board. As the city's largest supply of drinking water, Lake Purdy has limited recreational opportunities in order to minimize the possibility of contamination due to human activities. At many times of the year, particularly depending on how much the lake has been drawn down, Lake Purdy provides good birding. This lake has been known to be central Alabama's best magnet for usual species, particularly water birds. On the Water Board's property around the lake there is a fairly healthy colony of red-cockaded woodpeckers, but sighting one is not guaranteed. Access to the lake is somewhat limited. Shoreline birding is available at two points where roads cross part of the lake, and at a fish camp. At the fish camp, small boats can be rented, and if you want to see the lake and to check out its surrounding woods thoroughly, renting a boat is the best way to do it.

Despite the difficulty in getting to much of the lake and its fluctuating birding conditions, Purdy attracts some rare and unusual winter casuals and accidentals along with more common species of wintering waterfowl. Some of the rarer sightings have been greater scaup, white-winged scoter, snow goose, buff-breasted sandpiper, and red, Wilson's, and northern phalaropes. Various duck and goose species, eared grebe, and common loon have been sighted here. In Imhof's book *Alabama Birds*, he notes the dramatic decline of water birds in the Birmingham area, particularly Lake Purdy, from the 1944 to 1972 Christmas counts; this decline demonstrates the loss and degradation of available habitat. Call the AOS rare bird hotline, particularly during winter, to see if there is something at Lake Purdy warranting a special trip. White pelican has been found at Lake Purdy from time to time, and green-backed heron summers here. Wandering late summer/early autumn wood storks have also been sighted at the lake.

Lake Purdy is located along SH 119 North between US 280 and I-20. SH 119 can be reached from exit 246 (Cahaba Valley Road) off I-65, south of Birmingham. The intersection of SH 119 and US 280 is 9 miles from I-65; the back entrance to Oak Mountain State Park is located on SH 119, 5.7 miles from the interstate. Coming from US 280, head northeast on SH 119; after 2.4 miles, SH 119 crosses over an arm of the lake; watch for birds here. There are places to park on the north side of the road, on both sides of the bridge. One and a half miles past the arm of the lake, a short road to the left takes you to Lake Purdy Boat Dock, where you can get access to the lake and can rent small trolling boats. A fair portion of the lake is visible from this area. Grant's Mill Road (Jefferson County Road 143) leaves SH 119 1 mile past the road to the boat dock; this road goes north over another portion of the lake where one can watch for birds on the water. Grant's Mill Road crosses a bridge over the lake just 0.5 mile from SH 119; there is some parking on the south side of the bridge, but there are extensive parking areas north of the bridge and before the road turns away from the lake. Quite a bit of the lake can be scoped from here, and a fair amount of shoreline can be covered on foot.

# Chapter 4
# West Alabama and
# Tennessee Valley

## WILLIAM B. BANKHEAD NATIONAL FOREST

 Bankhead National Forest is located in the northwest portion of Alabama and contains some beautiful sandstone canyons which hold the largest trees in the state. The crowning jewel of the Bankhead is the 26,000-acre Sipsey Wilderness; the wilderness area is augmented by the Sipsey Fork Wild and Scenic River which protects more than 61 river miles of the Sipsey and its tributaries. Within these two areas, logging is no longer allowed and a rich and diverse hardwood forest is developing. Spring warblers here can be spectacular. The unique damp and cool conditions in the canyons encourage beech, tulip poplar, and eastern hemlock trees to grow to huge size and allow a wonderful mixture of songbirds which are usually easier to spot here than in other areas.

The Sipsey Wilderness is an ideal place for day hikes or for week-long backpacking outings. Deep in the heart of the area is Bee Branch, where the state's largest tree, a tulip poplar with a 22-foot circumference, is located. Many of the trails in the Sipsey go through expansive upland mixed hard-

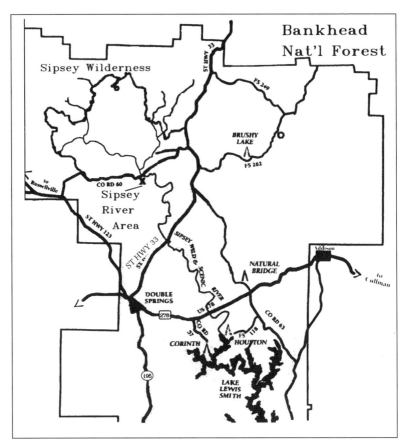

wood and pine forests, and the birding there can be good at times. However, it is in the cool, moist canyons that the best birding can be found. Describing the full trail system and the birding possibilities within the wilderness area are beyond the scope of this book, but the remote areas of canyon forest can provide you with a birding experience similar to the more accessible areas described below. If you want to combine a long backpacking trip with good birding, the Sipsey Wilderness area is your best bet in Alabama.

For those who are not inclined towards long hours of walking on wilderness trails, there are some wonderful canyon areas that are much more accessible. The best area is the Sipsey River recreation area on the Sipsey Fork. This is at the very southern end of the main trail system of the wilderness. The picnic area and parking lot is an excellent place to begin trips into the wilderness area or to bird in a beautiful canyon. Located right on the Sipsey Fork, south of the bridge where Winston County Road 60 crosses over the river, the picnic area is the loveliest I have ever seen. After turning off the county road, take the one-lane bridge over the river to the parking area. Just south of this parking area is an easy trail that goes south along the western bank of the

*Acadian Flycatcher*

river, and the picnic tables are along this trail. On the other side of the trail from the river is a high sandstone canyon wall, and the trail winds into a side canyon to a beautiful, 20-foot waterfall. Throughout this canyon are large beech, hemlock, and poplar trees, and I have had very good luck with spotting spring songbirds here, particularly in May. One can expect a variety of warblers, including northern parula, worm-eating, black-and-white, yellow-throated, cerulean, American redstart, hooded, and even Swainson's. Acadian flycatcher is relatively easy to find along the river banks, and I usually see a broad-winged hawk patrolling this stretch of the river. Eastern phoebe nest here. Belted kingfishers are common along the river. You can hike as far as you like along the river; when the water is low, it is easy to make your way south. At any time, there is a good trail (#209) to the north into the wilderness which takes you up the canyon of the Sipsey Fork. One half mile north, another trail (#200) branches into Borden Creek Canyon, which is another lovely ravine. Trails within the wilderness area are usually easy, but they have some very steep sections when going into or out of canyons, and some fording of creeks and the river is necessary at points. While not encompassing a large expanse, the Sipsey River picnic area is worth birding at a leisurely rate in the springtime and early summer. The songbirds can give quite a show, and even if not seen immediately, they fill the woods with their songs.

Another good location to look for warblers and flycatchers within a lovely canyon is the falls area on Hubbard Creek at the western edge of the wilderness area. A dirt road takes you to the side of this canyon, and a short, but steep, walk takes you into the canyon. There is a graceful waterfall that, with sufficient water, can double as a slide into a deep pool ideal for swimming on those hot, Alabama summer days.

Unfortunately, the beauty of this place has attracted people who swim and party here and then leave all their trash behind; every time I have been there, it has been spoiled by litter. Still, a short hike down the canyon is nice, and the same variety of songbirds are possible here, as well. I have found Acadian flycatchers to be particularly watchable here, often for long periods at minimum focus.

Natural Bridge is a very accessible spot that provides a nice canyon with an impressive natural bridge of sandstone across the upper portion of the canyon. This picnic area is just a mile north of US 278 on Winston County Road 63, and a short, 0.5 mile loop trail takes you into the canyon, under the bridge, up the far canyon wall, and back to the parking lot through an upland pine-hardwood forest. Various warblers can be found here in spring; in particular, look for worm-eating warblers foraging among the huge leaves of the big-leaf magnolia trees. Great crested flycatchers are common, and I have often encountered pairs of nesting tufted titmouse in hollow trees right along the trail before it descends into the canyon.

For more information about the Bankhead Forest and the Sipsey Wilderness and maps of the area, write Supervisor's Office, National Forests in Alabama, 2946 Chestnut Street, Montgomery, AL 36107.

## WHEELER DAM

On SH 101, north of US Alternate 72 and south of US 72, Wheeler Dam provides a good spot for viewing wintering birds on the Tennessee River. Birds that can be seen here include common loon (often in large numbers), hundreds of ring-billed gulls, American coot, great blue heron, belted kingfisher, and various ducks. This is a very wide dam, and a spotting scope is a much-needed tool for viewing the birds adequately. On rare occasions, Franklin's gull has been seen here.

On the southern side of the dam, there is a visitor's center and a good area for picnicking and for looking out over the water. The road crosses the dam, and there are parking lots on both sides of the road on the northern end of the dam. From the northern end of the dam, one can gain access to the walkways along the tops of the two locks; these walkways allow you to go some distance above and below the dam to look out over the water for birds. The simple rule at the dam is that if you have to open a gate, you cannot go there; all areas that do not require the opening of a gate to gain access to are open to the public. There are rest rooms available at the entrance to the locks.

Joe Wheeler State Park Resort is a major golf, marina, and recreation center that can provide some good views over Wheeler Lake; birds that can be seen at the dam may be seen here, but usually in smaller numbers. The entrance to the resort is located on US 72, 4.2 miles east of where SH 101 and US 72 intersect.

## WHEELER NATIONAL WILDLIFE REFUGE

Easily accessible from I-65, the Wheeler National Wildlife Refuge is located along the Tennessee River and includes much of the river and lake areas in its coverage. Wheeler is the largest national wildlife refuge in Alabama, with more than 34,500 acres. It is a major feeding area for migratory waterfowl, sometimes supporting 50,000 ducks and 30,000 Canada geese during the winter months. To get to the visitor center, take exit 334 off I-65 just south of where the interstate crosses the Tennessee River; go west on SH 67 North toward Decatur. Go 2.5 miles, and the entrance to the vis-

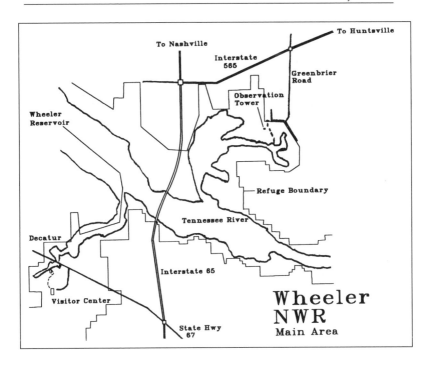

itor center will be on the left (south), where a short road takes you through fields to the parking lot. Look for meadowlarks and bluebirds in the fields. The refuge visitor center is very nice; it is open 10:00 a.m. through 5:00 p.m., Wednesday through Sunday.

Two trails lead from the visitor center. The trail to the observation building goes through some woods where small woodland birds can be seen. Look closely at any wrens seen, because Bewick's wren has been known to nest nearby and has been seen on the refuge. The observation building itself has to be one of the finest, most lavish blinds ever built; it is a two-story affair with heat and air-conditioning. With a set of bleachers in the main room, it can hold quite a crowd, and it is equipped with two spotting scopes. The main view is

*American Wigeon*

through a large window to the north, overlooking a pond where large numbers of ducks congregate in the winter. This pond is often seeded with corn to feed the birds, and it has fields on either side. Sometimes numbering in the thousands, the ducks on this pond can make a spectacular sight. Often seen are mallard, blue-winged teal, American wigeon, black duck, Canada goose, and American coot. Also possible here are bufflehead, canvasback, green-winged teal, redhead, ring-necked duck, lesser scaup, gadwall, northern shoveler, snow goose, pied-billed grebe, and various herons. There is a microphone set up on a pole in the middle of the lake, and speakers in the observation building allow you to hear the ducks. Mallard, black duck, wood duck, and Canada goose all nest on the refuge in small numbers.

South of the visitor center is a half-mile loop trail that takes you through a cypress swamp and alongside some fields. This is the Atkeson Cypress Trail, and it begins with a boardwalk through the swamp. Watch for hawks over the fields.

The refuge has a bird list with over 304 species on it. With its fortunate location, Wheeler has had a good share of accidental and unusual birds. Some of the rarities, at least for Alabama, that have been spotted at Wheeler include: red-throated loon, fulvous whistling duck, tundra swan, Ross's goose, Brant, barnacle goose, Egyptian goose, Eurasian wigeon, king eider, harlequin duck, surf scoter, white-winged scoter, masked duck, Swainson's hawk, rough-legged hawk, red knot, northern saw-whet owl, Sprague's pipit, Lapland longspur, red crossbill, and yellow-headed blackbird.

A great deal of the refuge is water, and another large portion is in fields that are managed to provide food and shelter for birds. One of the best places to observe birds in fields is on the north side of the river. Take I-565 east of I-65, towards Huntsville; exit 3 off I-565 is Greenbrier Road. Along Greenbrier Road are many fields, and this area attracts many hawks and kestrels. Take Greenbrier Road south 1.9 miles; then turn right on Pryor Road. Go through a small neighborhood; pass the Mount Zion Cumberland Presbyterian Church on the right. At an intersection where the paved road goes to the right, take the dirt road to the left; signs here indicate the refuge boundary. The road goes a short distance next to a field to an observation tower overlooking the surrounding fields. Here, you can look for hawks or watch waterfowl such as geese during the early winter months when there is plenty of feed left in the fields. The dirt road continues to the south a short ways until it dead-ends at a branch of Wheeler reservoir; wading birds and some waterfowl may be seen here. While driving the road south of the tower, watch for horned larks, which are common in winter in the two fields on either side of the road. Using your car as a blind, you can get very close up views of the larks.

There is much more to the refuge, but it is difficult for the public to gain access to, as many of the roads are closed. Having access to a boat will give one passage to most of the refuge, because the refuge covers much of the northern and southern shores of Wheeler Reservoir and some of its tributaries.

Information about Wheeler NWR and a bird list can be obtained by writing: Wheeler National Wildlife Refuge, Route 4, Box 250, Decatur, AL 35603. Being conveniently reached from one of the most direct routes south through Alabama, Wheeler is a natural stop for any birder headed south during the winter months.

## Decatur

Occasionally during the winter, there are invasions of more northerly species in the Decatur area. One area that attracts many of these species is the airport and ball fields at Calhoun Junior College. In the winter of 1991–92, a large number of Lapland longspurs (which are sighted most winters) with a few Smith's longspurs (the first in two decades) were regularly sighted here. To check this field, take US 31 north from Decatur, toward Athens; at the junction with US 72 that goes toward Huntsville, stay on US 31 heading north. At the first traffic light, Limestone County Road 45 (Airport Road) is immediately north of the Hardee's and bears to the right, straight to the fields, which are on the north side of the road, between one quarter and one half mile from the intersection. These fields include golf practice areas, a ballpark, and an airport that is used for pilot training. Also watch for horned larks and savannah sparrows.

## LAKE GUNTERSVILLE STATE PARK

Located on the western edge of Sand Mountain where it meets Lake Guntersville, this state park has become syn-

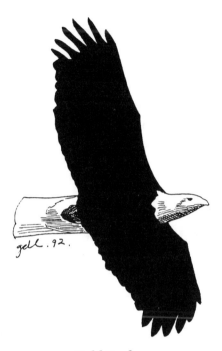

*Bald Eagle*

onymous with bald eagles. Every winter, as many as 75 to 100 bald eagles gather at Lake Guntersville. Most of them roost in Town Creek Canyon, which is part of the park. January is the best month for observing the eagles. "Eagle Weekend" tours have become very popular and are put on by the park every weekend during January. These tours include meals and lodging at the modern conference center, lectures on eagles and other raptors, and guided tours to see the eagles as they leave the roost in the morning, as they fish over the lake during the day, and as they return to the roost in the afternoon.

The park consists of 5,909 acres located on SH 227. From Guntersville, turn off US 431 onto SH 227; SH 227 goes over a causeway past an industrial area and then wind its way on into the park. A left turn off SH 227 takes you into the lodge/cabins/campground complex of the park; continuing on brings you to Town Creek, picnic areas, and then north out of the park. Lake Guntersville itself was formed by the damming of the Tennessee River and is over 66,000 acres in area; the lake is well known for its bass fishing.

Although the park is known widely for its eagles, Lake Guntersville has also traditionally been an excellent winter spot for ducks and other waterfowl. However, some foreign grass-eating carp were recently introduced into the lake and they are reducing the amount of water plants. As these plants decrease, so do the numbers of fish that have used the plants for food, shelter, and places to hide. With fewer fish, the lake has become less attractive to ducks and waterfowl, and to the eagles. As an example, in one day in January, 1988, I saw 75 eagles leave the roost in Town Creek Canyon during the morning, and I watched hundreds of pied-billed grebes, American coots, gadwalls, hooded mergansers, common goldeneyes, lesser scaups, and buffleheads on the lake. Rafts of several hundred coots together were not unusual. Common loons were plentiful on the lake, and sometimes they used to gather by the dozens and even the hundreds along the US 431 causeway leading north from the town of Guntersville. I even saw one snow goose. In January 1992, I saw only 16 eagles leave the roost, fifty coots, one loon, and one bufflehead; that was all. A friend saw a few dozen loons along the causeway. The release of the carp occurred after January 1988. Hopefully, conditions on the lake will return to a situation more favorable to birds soon.

Lake Guntersville State Park has a number of hiking trails that go up the mountainside and along the shore of the lake. Deer are extremely abundant and quite tame. In the woods of the park, during the winter one can find many bird species such as brown creeper, yellow-bellied sapsucker, golden-crowned kinglet, American goldfinch, northern junco, and pine siskin. In the pine woods around the cabins and the campgrounds, look for pine warbler, brown-headed nuthatch, song sparrow, Bachman's sparrow, and chipping sparrow. In summer, both scarlet and summer tanagers can be sighted in the hardwood forests. Check the sewage treatment pond beside the road to the campground for ducks. Great blue herons can almost always be found at the edge of the lake north of the picnic grounds on SH 227, north of Town Creek bridge, but also due to the carp, their numbers seems to be declining as well. Sometimes large numbers of wintering gulls gather on the lake, mostly ring-billed and herring gulls.

If your luck is not too good with the birds along the shore of the park, you can try the dam that forms the lake or the causeways that go into the town of Guntersville. Go back to Guntersville (watch for birds along the SH 227 causeway) and head north on US 431; the highway will cross over the lake on a combination bridge and causeway. On the northern end of the causeway, there are places to pull off the road. On the east side, Marshall County maintains a small park along the road. In winter, eagles, gulls, and loons (sometimes in the dozens and even hundreds) can be seen from the causeway, although there is no way to predict where the best spot along the causeway will be at any particular time. About 10 miles north of town, a road to the left leads to the dam. This road is marked with a sign and is 3.5 miles long. There are picnic areas and open fields next to the dam. Access to the walkways along the top of the locks is available to the public; these walkways stretch both above and below the dam to give views of the lake and river. Some eagles roost here during the winter, and recently, a pair set up a nest on the south bank. In winter, common loon, ring-billed gulls, and various species of duck can also be seen from the dam area. About midway from the highway to the dam, a road to the west (to the right, when headed toward the dam) goes through some privately owned fields. This is Hawk Farm. The owners of the farm will allow birders to stop along parts of this dirt road to watch for hawks and eagles. During January and other winter months, the huge fields here have provided homes to bald eagle, northern harrier, red-tailed hawk, and for several years, a rough-legged hawk. Other rarely seen raptors spotted here include merlin and prairie falcon. To reach Hawk Farm, take the dirt road on the right 2.7 miles from the intersection of the US 431 and the road to the dam. Go 0.7 mile to a wide area in the road where a shed and cattle pen are on the left; park there, and you will have a good vantage point over several hundred acres of fields with forest borders.

Information on attending an eagle weekend at the park can be obtained by writing: Lake Guntersville State Park, Alabama Highway 227, 1155 Lodge Drive, Guntersville, AL 35976-9126. Or, call the park at 205-582-2061.

## DESOTO STATE PARK AND MENTONE AREA

Rising higher than 2,000 feet and stretching for over eighty miles from Gadsden, Alabama, to Chattanooga, Tennessee, is flat-topped Lookout Mountain, an island in the sky covered with rolling farmlands and quiet woods. Often associated with Chattanooga and Civil War battles, Lookout Mountain is much more; only its northern end extends into Tennessee, and while part of it is in Georgia, most of the mountain is in Alabama. Along the top of Lookout Mountain runs the Little River, which has cut a canyon up to 700 feet deep out of the mountain: Little River Canyon. Together, the mountain and the canyon form a unique set of habitats that attracts many migratory birds and provides the southern-most extension of many species' summer ranges.

DeSoto State Park is accessible from several exits along I-59. Exit 231 takes you to Mentone and to the upper end of the park which includes DeSoto Falls and the headquarters section of the park alongside the Little River. From I-59, go east on SH 117 through Hammondville and Valley Head to Mentone. Turn right at the blinking light just as you reach Mentone, onto the Lookout Mountain Parkway. After three miles, a short road to the left leads to DeSoto Falls. On the parkway, continue south past Alabama's only snow skiing resort, Cloudmont. Follow the signs through two turns, the first to the left, the second to the right, and the road goes into the park where the headquarters, lodge, and campground are located. Continue south through the farms and fields on top of this mountain until you reach State Highway 35 from Fort Payne. Turn east on SH 35, proceed several miles, and cross over a bridge spanning the river just above Little River Falls. Park in the area immediately on the right after crossing the bridge. To go down the canyon, take the road heading south marked by a sign just to the west of the bridge on SH 35. The autumn colors along the roads of Lookout Mountain are often quite beautiful. Summers on the mountain and in Mentone are as pleasant as the weather ever gets anywhere in Alabama; the elevation keeps the temperatures surprisingly moderate. Also, in the winter this area is one of the few parts of Alabama that almost always get snow.

Birds that can be seen at all times in the Mentone area and at DeSoto State Park include tufted titmouse, Carolina chickadee, American goldfinch, white-breasted nuthatch,

*Black-throated Green Warbler*

eastern bluebird, and numerous varieties of woodpeckers. The pileated woodpecker is particularly easy to hear and spot in the woods around the headquarters of the park; try the hiking trails in that area.

Also present are winter residents such as yellow-bellied sapsucker, cedar waxwing, purple finch, golden-crowned and ruby-crowned kinglets, northern junco, and yellow-rumped warbler. When they are passing through, a most abundant species is the pine siskin. I have seen as many as 300 pine siskins at one time in the woods near the park.

Spring migrants that can be spotted are palm warbler, magnolia warbler, Canada warbler, and rose-breasted grosbeak. Summer residents in the park and the local woods include black-billed cuckoo, black-and-white warbler, cerulean warbler, worm-eating warbler, American redstart, ovenbird, Kentucky warbler, blue-gray gnatcatcher, and black-throated green warbler. Also look for summer and scarlet tanagers, blue grosbeak, and indigo bunting.

Nighttime birding can bring the calls of barred and great horned owls, and although it is rare in Alabama, a long-eared owl has been heard in the woods near Mentone.

Little River Canyon, which is part of DeSoto State Park, is spectacular. While the Little River has two forks that run over much of Lookout Mountain, the canyon itself begins at Little River Falls and courses ten miles before it ends on the southeast side of the mountain. The falls are encased in a bowllike cradle with sandstone walls; along these walls, many rough-winged swallows nest. The rims of the canyon are covered with laurel, with pines farther back, and the canyon itself contains a mixture of large hardwoods and pines. A road runs along the western rim of the canyon and provides a number of scenic vistas. From the falls, a trail follows the eastern rim of the canyon, and about 0.5 mile downstream descent into the canyon is possible. Pine warblers can be sighted in the tops of the pine trees rising out of the canyon. Watch the thickets for American woodcock moving through the brush away from the rim. Also look for Swainson's warbler and worm-eating warbler.

On the floor of the canyon, hooded warbler, eastern phoebe, and Louisiana waterthrush can be seen. Peregrine falcons have been seen on rare occasions in the canyon and patrolling the skies above. More likely to be seen over the canyon are broad-winged hawks.

Information on the park, campground, and rates for the lodge and cabins can be obtained by writing: Division of State Parks, Alabama Dept. of Conservation and Natural Resources, 64 North Union Street, Montgomery, AL 36130. Or you can call 1-800-ALA-PARK, nationwide. In 1992, Congress designated Little River Canyon as a national recreation area to be administered by the National Park Service.

The change in administration from the state to the Park Service had not yet occurred at the time of this writing.

The town of Mentone has a number of antique and craft shops where a small village atmosphere is preserved. At the main intersection in town are a beautiful Episcopal church, the Mentone Inn (a bed and breakfast), a crafts village with the Log Cabin Deli, and the historic Mentone Hotel, which is a large, rambling structure filled with various stores and shops.

# Mississippi

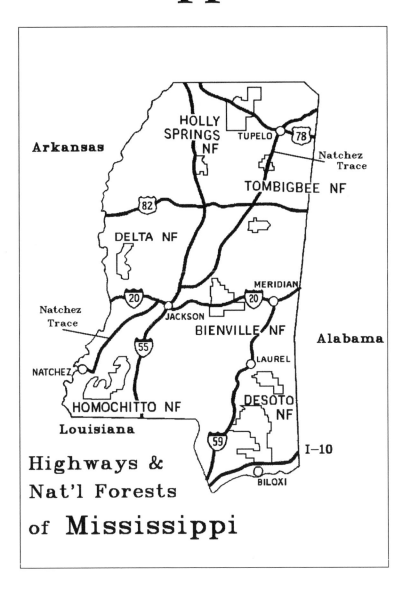

Highways &
Nat'l Forests
of Mississippi

# Chapter 5
# The Mississippi Coast

Birding along the coast of Mississippi has been covered in detail by Judith Toups and Jerome Jackson in their book *Birds and Birding on the Mississippi Coast,* published by the University Press of Mississippi. Their book goes into explicit particulars about birding locations in Hancock, Harrison, and Jackson Counties; details as specific as which roads in particular subdivisions to bird are included.

The purpose of this book is to give a general guide to the more accessible, public areas for bird watching over a two-state area. Therefore, I do not attempt to get as specific on the areas along the Mississippi coast. However, I have included the areas that I think will be the most productive for birds and the most accessible to the traveler. For those who wish to spend more time birding along the Mississippi coast or for those who live there, Ms. Toups and Mr. Jackson's book is highly recommended. The book is hardbound and retails for around twenty dollars; the address for the publisher is: University Press of Mississippi, Jackson, MS 39211.

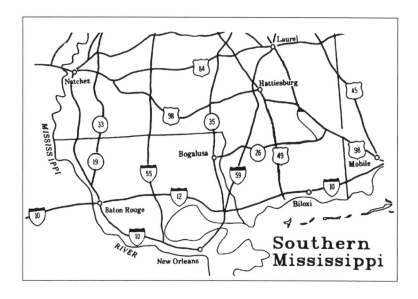

## GULF ISLANDS NATIONAL SEASHORE

Gulf Islands National Seashore is part of the National Park system; most of the park consists of barrier islands in the Gulf of Mexico off the Mississippi coast and portions of barrier islands in Florida. In Mississippi, there is one unit of the park that is onshore and very accessible; this is the Davis Bayou unit. Offshore, one can reach West Ship Island by ferry during the warmer months, and the other islands can be reached by private or chartered boat. Sheltered from the massive development that has occurred along most of the Gulf coast, these barrier islands provide a beautiful example of the primitive southern coast and make good places for watching for shore birds, migrants, and some pelagic birds.

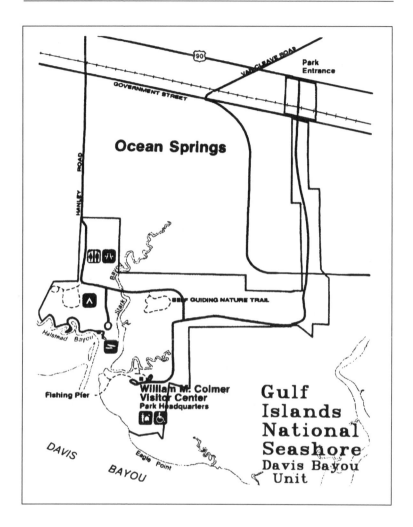

## Davis Bayou Unit

Located just east of Ocean Springs, the Davis Bayou unit of Gulf Islands National Seashore has many opportunities for observing the bird life found in the brackish marshes of this region. The entrance to the park is off the southern side of US 90, just east of the intersection of US 90 and Ocean Springs Road, where there is a traffic light; there is no traffic light at the entrance to the park, but there are signs. The entrance road will take you to the visitor center; park hours are 8:00 a.m. to 10:00 p.m., except for campers.

The visitor center has a number of displays about the park and some very interesting paintings and wood sculptures of the local scenes and wildlife. There are a number of short boardwalk trails around the visitor center that go through the woods and to overlooks of the marsh. From the southwest side of the parking lot, take the trail out to the fishing pier to get views of birds out in Davis Bayou. Look for brown pelicans, herons, egrets, wintering ducks such as red-breasted mergansers, grebes, gulls, and terns; the pier goes over part of the marsh as well.

In the marsh areas, look and listen for rails, particularly king, Virginia, and clapper rails. In spring, when low tide corresponds with dawn, one can see clapper and king rails come down to the waterline to bathe. During the month of June, clapper rails sometimes bring their young down to the waterline at low tide. From the boardwalks that overlook the marsh, stay quiet for a while and you may hear and see a marsh wren moving about in the reeds. Osprey and kingfisher sometimes fly over the marsh looking for food. Tricolored herons can be seen searching the shallow areas during low tide. There is a nature trail off the road leading to the campground; this trail goes through various woods and has a number of overlooks into the marsh. Marsh wren, rails, and Philadelphia vireo (in autumn) can be found here. The rest of the Davis Bayou Unit consists of picnic areas, a camping area, and a boat dock that provides more views of the marsh.

The whole Unit is not very large, but it is pretty and has been known to be a very good birding spot for spring migra-

*Marsh Wren*

tion. The woods around the picnic grounds and a informal trail along the western fence have been good areas during spring. Around the visitor center, those woods have also produced such birds as tanagers, orioles, and all the various warbler species that migrate through this area.

### West Ship Island

Excursion boats leave both Gulfport and Biloxi for West Ship Island during the months of March through October (from Gulfport) and from Memorial Day through Labor Day (from Biloxi). West Ship Island is about fifteen miles out from the Mississippi coast and has a well preserved Civil War fort. Fort Massachusetts has been known to harbor winter-

*Black Skimmer*

ing burrowing owls and has nesting barn swallows. Other birds that sometimes nest on the island include snowy plover, least tern, and black skimmer. The first stop for many spring migrants, this island can have occasionally large numbers of warblers, tanagers, buntings, and orioles. A boardwalk crosses over the salt marsh to the beach which has been rated as one of the ten best beaches in the country; mottled ducks have been seen in the pond next to the boardwalk.

The places to catch the excursion ferry to Ship Island are Gulfport Yacht Harbor, US 90 at US 49 (the phone number is 601-864-1014); and next to the Buena Vista Beach Club Inn in Biloxi, US 90 at the I-110 loop overpass (call 601-432-2197). The trip across Mississippi Sound takes a little over an hour, and the ride is a good opportunity to watch gulls and terns and to look for possible magnificent frigatebirds. Weekends can be crowded, and tickets go on a first-come, first-served basis; weekdays offer a much less crowded experience.

## Horn Island

Many diverse habitats occur on large Horn Island, making it an excellent location for birds. One reason it is so good for birds is that it is a designated wilderness area which is very inaccessible. There is a ranger station in the middle of the island, but other than that, there is no human presence on the entire island, and birds take full advantage of the ponds, marshes, forests, and beaches. The only way to reach Horn Island or any of the other islands in the National Seashore (other than West Horn Island) is by private boat, either your own or a charter. It can take days to explore all of Horn Island's habitats and bird species. Birds that have been seen on Horn Island include gray kingbird, burrowing owl, common moorhen, wintering ducks, wintering rails, gulls, terns, plovers, sandpipers, osprey, and peregrine falcon. In winter, northern gannet can be seen offshore, and pelagic birds such as magnificent frigatebird, masked booby, and brown booby have been sighted. For more particulars on Horn and the other remote islands and exactly where to go on each of them and which species to watch for, consult Toups and Jackson's book, which provides details about these islands.

Information on the national seashore, details on chartering boats, and a bird list containing 280 species sighted in the park can be obtained by writing: Superintendent, Gulf Islands National Seashore, 3500 Park Road, Ocean Springs, MS 39564.

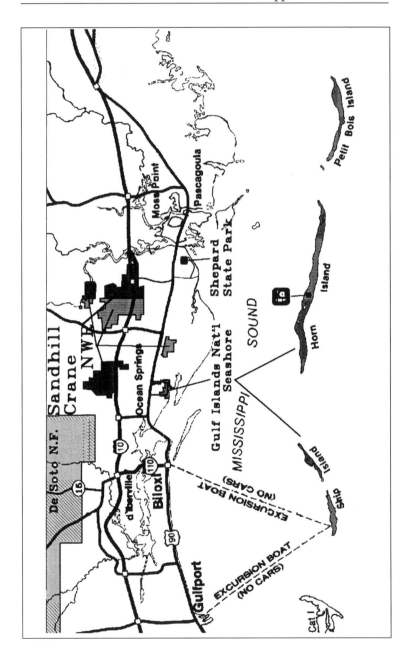

While in Ocean Springs, visit the Walter Inglis Anderson Museum, south of US 90 in the main part of town; follow the signs. Anderson was a local artist who spent much of his life studying and painting the local wonders of nature, particularly Horn Island. Sometimes, Anderson would row out to Horn Island alone and stay there for weeks at a time, surrounding himself with and studying the nature of the place. Anderson was a unique and talented individual. Parts of his home, which he decorated extensively with his art, are preserved in the museum. Some of his art representing the wildlife of the area is on display at the Davis Bayou visitor center.

## Shepard State Park

This convenient park in Gautier (pronounced go-shay) provides a mixture of woodlands and marsh. Part of the park is developed for group recreation and for RVs and camping, but toward the northern end of the park, there is a picnic area from which trails go out into the pine/oak woods and along the bank of the marsh. Wood ducks can be seen in the small stream at the start of the trail. After crossing a small bridge, the trail divides three ways; the trail to the left (south) leads along the shore of the marsh and comes to an overlook into the marsh. Continuing on this trail takes you into the woods where a series of trails wind through the forest. All of these trails circle around to reconnect with each other.

Seaside, sharp-tailed, savannah, swamp, and Bachman's sparrows winter here; during that season, also look for rusty blackbird and rails, particularly king rail, in the marsh. Spring and fall migrants can occur here, but it is not one of the best spots for consistently finding them. Groove-billed ani has been seen here in spring and fall.

The park entrance is on the north side of Graveline Road, 1.5 miles east of its intersection with Ladnier Road, which turns south off US 90 just east of where the Gautier-Vancleave Road (the road going south from exit 61 on I-10) hits US 90. There is an entrance fee. Inside the park there are named, gravel roads; take Navaho Road until it dead-ends at Mohawk Road. Go left to the picnic area; the trails begin at the southern end of this area.

## Gulf Marine State Park

Turn south on Myrtle Street, at the first light on US 90 west of the bridge from Ocean Springs to Biloxi, to find Gulf Marine State Park. This small park gives you views out over the pass between Biloxi and Ocean Springs and Biloxi Bay.

## Least Tern Nesting Area

Large numbers of endangered least terns nest during the spring and early summer on a portion of the beach near Gulfport. As many as 6,000 pairs nest here, making this the largest nesting colony of least terns in the world. The sight of these birds on the beach and swirling overhead is quite impressive. Be sure to watch from a distance so as not to disturb the birds and to avoid having your head dive-bombed by irritated terns. US 90 goes right by the nesting area, and if you travel this road in the early summer, the nesting area on the south side of the highway is impossible to miss; there are fences and signs marking the areas. The terns also nest east of US 49 in Gulfport, between Courthouse Road Pier and the Broadwater Marina in Biloxi. Watch for fish crows which raid the colony for eggs to eat. June and July are the best times for observing the nesting terns.

The entire beach in Harrison County from Pass Christian to Biloxi is more than 25 miles long. To make stops at turnoffs along the road, it is best to be traveling from west to east, as the beach and the turnoffs are on the south side of the highway. The beach is quite wide in places, and groups of shorebirds can occur anywhere along its length. Black skimmers, numbering in the hundreds at times, can be seen on the beach.

### Buccaneer State Park

Located in Waveland, on the western portion of Mississippi's coast, Buccaneer State Park is a basically developed park, but it does have some trails and some beach area that can occasionally provide good birding. The developed portion of the park is on the northern side of Beach Road, and the Gulf of Mexico is immediately across the road. Depending on wave action and the tides, there will be more or less beach to bird upon. In the park itself, there are nature trails through some woods and alongside a tidal marsh; these are the nature trails leaving from the comfort station near the main entrance and the Old Hickory Nature Trail (where the marsh is) at the day-use area entrance, just east of the main entrance. A short trail called Pirates Paradise Nature Trail is near the activity building. Spring migration can bring a fair number of warblers, orioles, tanagers, and other migrants through the woods of the park; however, there are better places to find such migrants.

The area in and around Buccaneer State Park was used by the notorious Jean Lafitte in the late 1700s as a base for his smuggling and pirating operations along the Gulf coast.

Later, Andrew Jackson used the site as a base of military operations during the Battle of New Orleans. The park has campgrounds, picnic areas, a wave pool, and tennis courts. The park address is Buccaneer State Park, 1150 S. Beach Boulevard, Waveland, MS 39576. To reach the park, turn south off US 90 at the sign near where US 90 intersects with SH 43; proceed south on Nicholson Avenue. After about 1.5 miles, cross some railroad tracks and make an immediate right (there is a sign) onto Central Avenue. Come to a four-way stop intersection; turn left onto Coleman Avenue. Go through the main part of Waveland, and the street will dead-end at the beach onto Beach Road (also called Beach Boulevard). Turn right (there is a sign), and the park entrances will be on the right, the day-use area first, and then the main entrance.

## MISSISSIPPI SANDHILL CRANE NATIONAL WILDLIFE REFUGE

The Mississippi Sandhill Crane National Wildlife Refuge is located along I-10 in southern Mississippi. To reach the headquarters and visitor center, take exit 61 onto Gautier-Vancleave Road and go north about 0.5 mile; the entrance road is to the right with an information booth just past the entrance. A short drive brings you to the visitor center where there are daily slide shows and films about the cranes. The visitor center and the road to it are open 8:00 a.m. to 3:00 p.m., Monday through Friday; closed on weekends.

Behind the visitor center is a 0.75 mile nature trail that takes you past some beautiful bayou swamps and through a pine savannah. The crane is an endangered subspecies of the sandhill crane, and there are only about 100 Mississippi Sandhill cranes left. The entire refuge comprises three units

*Sandhill Crane*

that cover more than 19,000 acres, so, seeing one of the cranes can be a matter of luck. Nonetheless, the refuge is a lovely area that preserves a habitat that has been mostly lost along the Gulf coast. During January and February, the refuge personnel will take groups out to blinds for a better chance to observe the cranes. Call ahead for arrangements: 601-497-6322. Although the chances of seeing a crane here are low, this refuge gives one the best spot in Alabama and Mississippi to attempt to see Sandhill cranes, as the members of this subspecies remain at the refuge year-round.

While on the trail, look for the other bird species that frequent the refuge; these include most of the herons and egrets native to the region. In the open pine savannahs, pine warblers and brown-headed nuthatches are common. In the brushy areas near the visitor center, watch for sedge wrens, which nest on the refuge. During winter, Lincoln's sparrow may also be spotted near the visitor center. Some other birds seen on the refuge include snow goose, fulvous whistling duck, swallow-tailed kite, ferruginous hawk, and long-billed dowitcher. During spring migration, any of the migrating warbler, tanager, bunting, and oriole species are possible, but as the refuge is landward of their first landfall, sighting these migrants here is largely a matter of luck.

A portion of I-10 runs through two of the units, and you can see signs identifying the refuge in the pine woods just past the fence along the highway. Also, the two rest areas (for eastbound and westbound traffic) at the western end of the bridge over the West Pascagoula River are good places to stop to watch for marsh birds and for hawks over the marshes and river. These rest stops are in part of the Gautier Unit of the refuge, where it abuts the river.

For more information on the refuge, write Mississippi Sandhill Crane National Wildlife Refuge, U.S. Fish and Wildlife Service, 7200 Crane Lane, Gautier, MS 39553. An informative brochure with a map of the refuge units is available.

# Chapter 6
# Central Mississippi

## DESOTO NATIONAL FOREST

 DeSoto National Forest offers the best hiking and canoeing opportunities in the national forests of Mississippi. The state's only two designated wilderness areas are in this national forest, and Mississippi's premier national wild and scenic river is also here. Generally located along US 49, the main unit of the forest provides a number of good birding spots.

### Leaf Wilderness

One of the smallest units of the national wilderness system, at 940 acres the Leaf Wilderness offers little chance for true solitude and wild adventure. However, it is a very accessible little area that preserves a beautiful bottomland hardwood swamp and some surrounding ridgelines. The ridges consist primarily of loblolly and shortleaf pine, some quite large, and the rest of the area is in the floodplain of the Leaf River and has a forest of various oaks, sweetgum, and cypress. During spring, warblers and other songbirds sing and nest,

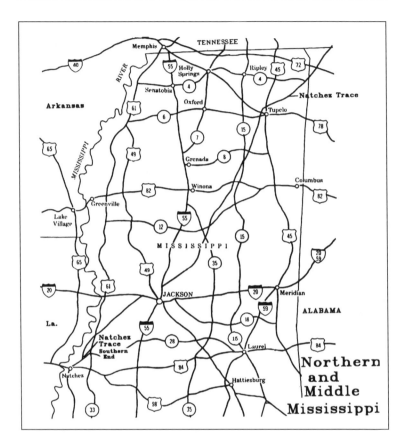

but the density of the forest often means that these birds are heard rather than seen. Prothonotary warbler, pine warbler, northern parula warbler, hooded warbler, yellow-throated warbler, Swainson's warbler, red-eyed vireo, yellow-throated vireo, and Louisiana waterthrush may be found here. Insects can be bad in warm weather.

To reach the Leaf Wilderness, go south from McClain on SH 57; from the intersection where SH 57 splits off from US 98, it is 7 miles to a parking area on the left (east) where the

Leaf Trail goes into the wilderness area. This trail winds around the southern part of the area and then heads north into the floodplain.

## Black Creek Wilderness

Located east of SH 29 and north of Wiggins, Black Creek Wilderness is 5,000 acres of preserved forest along Black Creek. Black Creek Trail runs through the wilderness area and is the best way to access the area on land. A canoe float trip down Black Creek is also a good way to see this place. The bird life here is typical for the area and habitats and is fairly plentiful along the creek. In spring, watch for acadian flycatcher, belted kingfisher, northern parula warbler, prothonotary warbler, hooded warbler, red-eyed vireo, summer tanager, and many other forest songbirds.

A parking area (called Janice Landing) on the northern side of the SH 29 bridge over Black Creek provides good access to the creek. Black Creek Trail enters the wilderness from the highway about 0.5 mile south of the bridge, where there is a parking area on the west side of the road. Black Creek Trail generally follows the creek and is a total of 41 miles, of which only 10 miles are in the wilderness area. The southern terminus of the trail is at Fairley Bridge Landing, and the northern end of the trail is at Big Creek Landing. There are campgrounds at both areas.

A float trip down Black Creek through the wild and scenic river area also begins at Big Creek Landing and ends at Fairley Bridge Landing; the 21 miles from Moody's Landing to Fairley is the designated wild and scenic part. This float trip can be cut into smaller segments, but the total length of creek that can be run between those two main points is 40 miles.

## Pitcher Plant Bog

One of the ecosystems unique to the South's coastal plain is the pitcher plant bog. Alabama and Mississippi were once blessed with thousands of acres of bogs, but most have been converted into pine plantations and farm land. In DeSoto National Forest is a very accessible and wildly beautiful bog that must not be missed if you are here in the early spring or summer. Pitcher plants are carnivorous plants that consume bugs to supplement the poor nutrient conditions provided by the soil they live in. These bogs contain many other species of plants particular to this habitat type besides the pitcher plants, and specialized insects as well. From SH 26, east of Wiggins, it is less than a mile to a spectacular bog of several hundred acres. At the intersection of SH 26 and SH 15, SH 15 goes south; take Forest Road 373 north from this intersection. Pitcher plant bogs will be visible on both sides of the road, and after just 0.5 mile, a huge bog will be on the west side of the road. The plants bloom in early and mid-April with large, lovely yellow flowers. Although there is nothing unusual about the birding here, the size and beauty of this bog give you a view of one of the nation's most amazing ecosystems which is now all too rare.

## Tuxachanie Hiking Trail

This 21.5 mile trail provides more opportunities for getting into the woods and watching birds. Pitcher plant bogs can be seen along parts of the trail, as well as pine savannahs, which used to cover so much of southern Mississippi; the trail also passes swamps and a number of small ponds. To see the pitcher plants in bloom, mid-April is the best time to hike this trail. Birds along the trail will be typical for this area; the longleaf and slash pine forests dominate here, and are good habitat for brown-headed nuthatch, pine warbler, and various woodpeckers. Foraging red-cockaded woodpeckers are pos-

*Brown-headed Nuthatch*

sible, but very unlikely. The western trailhead for this trail is right on the east side of US 49, between the towns of Saucier to the south and McHenry to the north; look for the rows of live oaks. The trail can also be accessed from Airey Lake recreation area which is reached by taking SH 67 east from Saucier and then going north 3 miles on Forest Road 412.

## Red-cockaded Woodpecker Colony

A very accessible colony of these endangered woodpeckers was set out in Jackson and Toup's book on birding coastal Mississippi, and as of 1993, that colony was still active. Three nesting trees are located directly on a paved road east from SH 15. Take Forest Road 402 (the Larue Road) east from SH 15; it is not marked, but it is a three-way intersection that is 13.2 miles north of where the two-lane part of SH 15 heads north from the east-west, four-lane portion of SH 15, just north of its intersection with I-10 and I-110. Go 2.65 miles and the colony will be on the right (south); park at an old road turnout on the north side of the road about 0.1 mile further east. The colony trees are marked with two blue bands of paint, and the colony area is marked by trees with one blue band of paint. Due to their foraging throughout a wide area during the day, the woodpeckers are rarely seen at these trees unless one gets there before dawn and waits for them to wake up at sunrise.

For more information, a map of the forest and excellent maps of the wilderness areas and trails, write to Forest Supervisor, National Forests in Mississippi, 100 W. Capitol Street, Suite 1141, Jackson, MS 39269.

## HOMOCHITTO NATIONAL FOREST

Homochitto National Forest is located in southwestern Mississippi along US 84 and was the first national forest in Mississippi. Like many other national forests in this state, Homochitto is a patchwork mixture of federal and private lands, and few nonhunting recreational opportunities are available. The best spot to camp, hike, and bird is around Clear Springs Lake, which is about 4 miles south of consolidated US 84/98, almost halfway between Roxie and Bude. There are prominent signs showing the way to the lake down County Road 104. US 84/98 is a four-lane road at the point where CR 104 goes south for 3.8 miles to the lake recreation area.

There is a short hiking trail around the lake and among the camping areas. A new (built in 1991 and 1992) trail begins just north of the entrance to the Clear Springs Lake recreation area and takes a 10.5-mile loop route through the mostly pine forest, past several small streams. A map showing the route of the trail is at the trailhead; hopefully, a trail map will soon be available to the public. This trail provides easy walking and is the best opportunity for birding in this

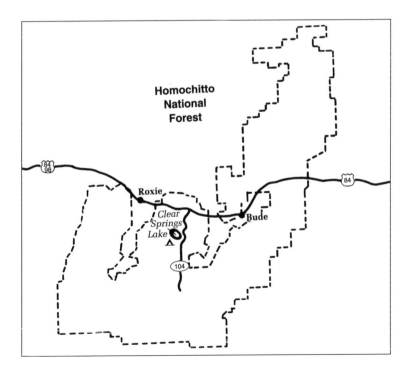

forest. While red-cockaded woodpecker is a remote possibility, one is more likely to spot the common pine woodland birds of this area: brown-headed nuthatch, pine warbler, pileated woodpecker, the other local woodpecker species, white-eyed vireo, Carolina wren, Carolina chickadee, great-crested flycatcher, and others.

For more information and a map of the forest, write to Forest Supervisor, National Forests in Mississippi, 100 W. Capitol Street, Suite 1141, Jackson, MS 39269.

## NATCHEZ TRACE PARKWAY

Running from near Natchez, Mississippi, to near Nashville, Tennessee, the Natchez Trace Parkway follows a historic route important to the development of our nation. As a unit of the National Park system, the parkway provides some of the most beautiful driving in the country. Although not as well known as the Blue Ridge Parkway, the Natchez Trace is a roadway deserving of great praise. The majority of the parkway is in Mississippi, with a small portion in the northwest corner of Alabama, and no other road makes these two states look so good. With parts of the roadway and its surrounding lands having been protected since the 1930s, the fields and forests alongside the parkway have been preserved to develop into a maturity and beauty lacking almost everywhere in the remaining parts of these two states.

From approximately 1800 to 1830, the Natchez Trace was used by farmers of the middle Tennessee area in order to return home after bringing their goods down the Mississippi River to market in Natchez. The farmers would build longboats to carry their crops to Natchez; once they arrived, they would sell the crops. Because it was very difficult to pole the boats back upriver, they dismantled the boats, sold the wood, and walked or rode horseback up the Natchez Trace to their homes in middle Tennessee. The early years of this era showed the travelers great hardship with few provisions or waystations on the route and ready highwaymen lurking along the way. Nonetheless, the Trace was the best way back to Tennessee. The Trace had a prior history as an Indian trail and a route of the pioneering traders, and after the days of the boatmen were over, the Trace was used as a post road and a military road.

Nowadays, this route is a scenic parkway, and the pre-served areas along it provide a number of special birding opportunities. One can bird practically the length of Mis-sissippi by traveling this single road. Spring brings wild-flowers, particularly dogwood, and northbound migrant bird species; autumn brings lovely colors to the hardwoods, and southbound migrants. Taking a few days to travel the Natchez trace through Mississippi and Alabama can be a very worthwhile trip.

The Trace goes through countless woodlands, both pine and hardwood, and through many fields and pastures. Any of the wooded areas are likely spots for the woodland species that occur in this area, and the open areas should be watched for eastern meadowlark, northern bobwhite, eastern bluebird, loggerhead shrike, and eastern kingbird; also look for horned lark, hawks, and kestrels in the winter. Scan the bare fields for water pipit in winter. Be careful while driving as deer are common along and on the road, and deer–car collisions are one of the major sources of accidents along the Trace.

Although there are many more areas along the Trace to stop and to do some birding, the following spots are my favorites, and they will give you a good sampling of the var-ious habitats along the route. I have arranged this listing in a south-to-north direction of travel, as that is the way the Trace was originally traveled and it is the way the roadway's mileage is numbered. As the Park Service has not yet completed acquisition and construction of three segments of the parkway, some mileages simply do not exist yet. The three missing pieces of the parkway are the first few miles at Natchez, the route through Jackson, and the final miles near Nashville. The parkway begins at mile 8.1, the temporary terminus near Natchez. Because it is such a small portion of the Trace and because I wish to treat the parkway as a unit, I am including the Alabama portion of the parkway here in the Mississippi section of the book.

## Natchez State Park: Mile 10.3

SH 553 crosses the Trace; the eastern branch goes to Natchez State Park, while the western portion goes to Emerald Mound. SH 553 crosses US 61 after 0.75 mile and then continues on to the park. After a short distance, the road forks with the campground to the right and the lake and picnic area to the left. Reaching the lake requires passing over a narrow, old bridge that cannot handle heavier vehicles. The lake has some hardwoods around it, and the picnic area is in a pecan orchard. Eastern kingbird, eastern pewee, common nighthawk, rough-winged swallow, and eastern bluebird can be found here. The birding here has not been very good for me, but it is worth a try during spring migration.

## Emerald Mound: Mile 10.3

Located about a mile west of the Trace, Emerald Mound is the second largest Indian mound still in existence. Taking up almost eight acres, the mound is a large, grassy platform upon which one can look into the canopies of the surrounding forest and over the trees; a short trail leads to the top of the mound and to the top of a secondary, temple mound on top of the larger one. This is a good place to watch for passing hawks, kites, egrets, and herons that may be headed to or from the nearby Mississippi River to the west. At any rate, this mound is an impressive sight.

### Rocky Springs: Mile 54.8

A major campsite and stopping area on the Trace, Rocky Springs contains over 0.5 mile of the original Trace along which one can walk through mature woodland. There is also a trail alongside Little Sand Creek, and together, these trails give you good chances to see woodland birds and to experience part of what it was like to walk the original Trace.

### Sunken Trace: Mile 104.5

Although there are a number of places along the Trace where you can see portions of the old, original trail, this stop has been the most productive for birds, in my experience. A small field borders some woods that contain part of the original Trace; it is a trail eroded into the ground by the many feet that passed this way long ago. The trees here are quite large, and I have seen in these trees more than one hundred warblers and vireos at once during early April. Most were yellow-rumped warblers, yellow-throated warblers, white-eyed vireos, and yellow-throated vireos, but their numbers and their height up in the trees kept me from identifying many of them. Perhaps by chance, I have found more birds available in spring and summer here than I have at other similarly sized areas on the Trace.

## Reservoir Overlook: Mile 105.6

This overlook on top of a hill gives you a good view out over Ross Barnett Reservoir, alongside which the Trace goes for about eight miles. Double-crested cormorant, Canada goose, and various duck species can be seen on the lake during winter.

Note: Highway 43: Mile 114: Highway 43 east will take you a short distance to Pearl River waterfowl refuge and Ross Barnett Reservoir (discussed later in this chapter).

## Cypress Swamp: Mile 122.0

Leading through a truly impressive cypress and tupelo swamp in an old portion of the Pearl River, this trail includes boardwalks that give easy and excellent views of prothonotary warblers and Louisiana waterthrushes in the early summer. Watch the trees for the warblers and the waterline for the waterthrushes. Numerous great-crested flycatchers can be found here, and the trail goes through a wooded area to an arm of the river for views over water and over marshes. The marshes are a good spot to listen for king rail, and the woods between the swamp and the river seem to be a focal point for migrants headed to more northern areas. Migrants such as magnolia warbler can be found here until quite late in the spring migration. Summer tanager and red-headed woodpecker are common in these woods. Watch the skies over the river for possible Mississippi kites in summer.

## Myrick Creek: Mile 145.1

This area displays the effects that beavers have had on the landscape, and the swampy bottomlands here are a regular spot for prothonotary warbler, pine warbler, red-bellied woodpecker, white-eyed vireo, and other woodland species.

## Hurricane Creek: Mile 164.3

Various soil conditions are encountered along this short trail as it goes through bottomlands and up to a dry ridge. The woods here collect migrants; I have spotted Swainson's thrush here during spring migration.

## Cole Creek: Mile 175.6

This short trail leads through a tupelo/bald cypress swamp. Prothonotary warbler is a regular here during the spring and summer.

## Jeff Busby Site: Mile 193.1

This is a major service area at about the midpoint in the Trace; a gas station, convenience store, telephone, restrooms, picnic grounds, and campsites are available. A road goes up to Little Mountain to give you views in two directions over the pine and hardwood forests of the area. A very nice nature trail emphasizing edible plants, and a further trail that goes back to the campground both start at the overlooks. The nature trail descends into a hollow, to a spring, and overlooks the tree canopies of a very pretty hardwood forest that includes some large white oaks. In spring and summer, watch for orioles and warblers, which are heard much more often than they are seen.

## Pigeon Roost: Mile 203.5

This is a historic site for birders. This spot used to be the roosting area for millions of passenger pigeons, which are now extinct. Here we are reminded how much we have lost of the natural world and America's original bird life, and how we must work to prevent the loss of any more species.

## Tombigbee National Forest

Between mile markers 233 and 248, the Trace passes through a portion of the Tombigbee National Forest. Although only slightly possible, this area is probably one's best bet for seeing red-cockaded woodpeckers along the Trace. The Trace has protected the pine trees along its route for over 60 years, but most of the Trace does not have enough of these older trees together in an area large enough to support the woodpeckers. Here, in the national forest section of the roadway, the odds are a bit better. As for venturing into the forest itself, a side road at mile marker 243.1 will take you to Davis Lake, a pleasant picnicking and summer camping area with a few short trails around the lake.

## Dogwood Bottom: Mile 275.2

Here, a portion of the original Trace can be found along with some dogwood trees more than one hundred years old, the largest I have ever seen. The woods in this small hollow are very beautiful in the early spring with the thousands of white dogwood blossoms. Birding here is much the same as in other hardwood areas along the parkway, but the old dogwoods are definitely worth a stop, particularly when in bloom.

## Donivan Slough: Mile 283.3

A short nature trail takes you through bottomland hard-woods along a slough and the adjacent flood plain. There are bald cypress trees along with water oak, tulip poplar, sycamore, black willow, and swamp chestnut oak. Winter brings a number of yellow-bellied sapsuckers to this wood, and spring brings in several swamp warblers and other songbirds such as hooded warbler, Kentucky warbler, and indigo bunting.

## Pharr Mounds: Mile 286.7

This 90-acre open area contains an impressive complex of eight Indian mounds of varying sizes. The mounds are evoca-tive and the extensive, open, grass field gives an excellent chance to spot grassland birds along the northern portion of the Trace. This is a good spot for hawks, meadowlark, red-winged blackbird, and swallows, and for horned lark and east-ern phoebe in winter. In spring, the wind blowing the wild-flowers and grasses into waves is a beautiful sight.

## Tenn-Tom Waterway: Mile 293.2

Park on the northern side of the bridge and walk to the edge of the Tennessee-Tombigbee Waterway. From here, an excellent view of the Bay Springs Lake lock and dam is immediately upstream. The grassy areas around the parking area have many pretty wildflowers and offer the best closeup views of the aerial acrobatics of cliff swallows and barn swal-lows I have ever seen. During spring and early summer, dozens of swallows will fly within feet of you, which makes tracking them with your binoculars very easy and exciting.

## Tishomingo State Park: Mile 302.8

With the Trace going right through this park, it is ideally situated for a visit. Tishomingo has 13 miles of trails through its expansive hardwood forest, and that trail system makes for excellent woodland birding possibilities. The park also has a large lake, a lodge, cabins, a campground, playing fields, and picnicking areas. A special feature of this park is that twice daily from April through mid-October, the park offers eight-mile float trips down Bear Creek, which runs through the preserve. The trips are pleasant during the warm weather here and give one the chance to watch for birds without having to work up a sweat walking down a trail.

More information about Tishomingo can be gotten by writing Tishomingo State Park, P.O. Box 880, Tishomingo, MS 38873.

## Cave Spring: Mile 308.4

Located in a group of hardwood trees in the midst of open fields, Cave Spring is lovely and cool grotto in a sinkhole. The usual woodland and field birds may be spotted here. Summer tanager appears to be a summer regular here.

## Bear Creek Mound: Mile 308.8

Just before crossing into Alabama, there is another Indian mound; this one was built between 1200 and 1400 A.D. This mound is relatively small and is in a small open field next to some woods.

## Freedom Hills Overlook: Mile 317.0

A steep, paved trail 0.25 mile long takes you to the highest point on the Trace; at an elevation of 800 feet you can look out over the parkway and the hills of northwestern Alabama. The woods here have a greater mix of pines, and pine warbler is common; blue-gray gnatcatcher can be seen along the trail. The overlook provides a bench and a good spot to watch for hawks during winter and also during spring and fall migrations.

## Buzzard Roost Spring: Mile 320.3

This small area of bottomland hardwoods contains a spring that flows from under a limestone outcropping. It is a very pretty little spot, and the field at the entrance usually has several eastern bluebirds foraging about.

## Tennessee River: Mile 328

There are places to stop on both sides of the river, and both areas provide more woodland habitat to search as well as good views over the water. Winter is a good time to check for ducks, herons, gulls, and common loon out on the river.

## Rock Spring: Mile 330.2

This short trail takes you through an old field that is growing up with hardwoods and along a very pretty stream. The stream, Colbert Creek, is fed by Rock Spring and has several beaver ponds on it; the water is very cool and clear with plenty of fish and turtles visible. The trail crosses the stream over some well-designed stepping stones and then

*Ruby-throated Hummingbird*

goes up to the spring. Belted kingfisher, great crested fly-catcher, and indigo bunting can be seen along the stream banks. Past the spring, the trail goes up a hillside to some limestone bluffs and through the forest. There are good views of the canopy of the trees further down the hill. Spring and summer can reveal northern oriole, Acadian flycatcher, summer tanager, Carolina wren, yellow-throated vireo, black-and-white warbler, American redstart, and cerulean warbler. Although the heavy foliage makes it easier to hear the birds rather than to see them, I have found spring and early summer here to be an exciting time with many possi-bilities. On my visits, the woods were thriving with bird life. In the fall, the orange blossoms of the jewelweed attract southbound ruby-throated hummingbirds.

## BIENVILLE NATIONAL FOREST

Bienville National Forest is located on I-20 east of Jackson. Encompassing 178,000 acres, the forest is a patchwork mixture of federal and private lands, and very little non-hunting recreational opportunities are available. However, Bienville offers perhaps the most accessible site available for seeing the red-cockaded woodpecker.

### Bienville Pines Scenic Area

The Bienville Pines Scenic area is just two miles from I-20, and it contains the largest stand of old-growth pine in Mississippi. The fact that this area of large, impressive pine trees is only 180 acres emphasizes the sad fact that human beings have eliminated virtually all of the natural environments that existed in the eastern United States. Further, the

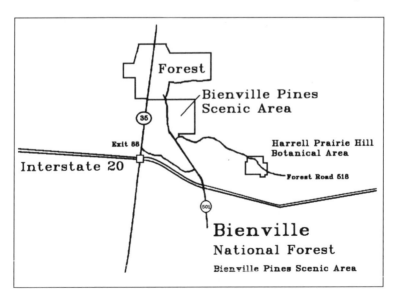

pines in this 180-acre area are intensively managed; pine bark beetle infested trees are cut down, and hardwoods near the woodpecker areas are cut to open those areas for the birds. Despite the large size and impressive age of the trees(some are over 200 years old), the area is not a scenic wonder. It is between the town of Forest and I-20, and the sound of vehicles and other human devices is constant. Also, a natural gas pipeline dissects the area. Nonetheless, there are big pines, and red-cockaded woodpeckers live here. Although you may see the woodpeckers anywhere in the area, the best place I have found is at the easternmost segment of the looping trail that runs through the tract. There are numbered signs along the trail which correspond to a trail guide. However, the trail guide is often not available at the trailhead. Follow the trail to an area of many tall pines where the hardwoods in the understory have been girdled and cut down. Several red-cockaded woodpecker nest trees are visible in this area, and at a bend in the trail, guidepost number 7 provides a good view of this stretch of trees. Wait, and listen for the distinctive call of the woodpeckers. I witnessed a pair of the woodpeckers mating here.

Other species of woodpeckers are also common in Bienville Pines, as well as pine warblers. However, other than the good sightings of red-cockaded woodpeckers, the birding here has never been very prolific for me.

To reach Bienville Pines Scenic Area, take exit 88 off I-20, and go north on SH 35. After just 0.1 mile, a road goes right (east) to connect with SH 501. This road's intersection with SH 35 has a Day's Inn and a Shell station on the northeast corner; there is a Best Western on the southeast corner. In less than a mile, this road dead-ends into SH 501; SH 501 is not marked here; turn left (north). In 0.2 mile, Forest Road 518 turns off to the right; this is the way to Harrell Prairie

*Red-cockaded Woodpecker*

(see next section). In another 0.4 mile going north on SH 501, the parking area for Bienville Pines is on the right; a church is immediately across from the parking lot on the west side of the road.

## Harrell Prairie Hill Botanical Area

Take Forest Road 518 (which is dirt) east from SH 501 for 2 miles to an open area along the top of a hill. This is an area managed to preserve the unique plant life that represents some of the prairie that once existed throughout more of this part of Mississippi. The area is burned in the late winter, and early April provides a very pretty show of wildflowers. With the open spaces, this is a good area to watch for hawks and eastern bluebirds. There is no parking area; pull off the road as best you can. The road is wide enough here to allow even a large truck to pass if a car is parked on the side.

Bienville National Forest does have one major trail, the Shockloe Trail, which is 23 miles long. However, this trail is designed primarily for horseback riding.

For more information and a map of the forest, write to Forest Supervisor, National Forests in Mississippi, 100 W. Capitol Street, Suite 1141, Jackson, MS 39269.

## Roosevelt State Park

On the western edge of Bienville National Forest is Roosevelt State Park. This is a small park around a lake. It is easily reached by taking exit 77 on I-20 and then going north. Camping is available here; birding should be representative of the area in general, with such species as eastern bluebird, pine warbler, eastern pewee, blue-gray gnatcatcher, and, in winter, hermit thrush.

## PEARL RIVER WATERFOWL REFUGE

Run by the Mississippi Department of Conservation on Ross Barnett Reservoir, this waterfowl area is a good birding spot during winter. A series of impoundments provide shallow wetlands for the birds, and the lake provides deep water habitat. There are few places to park, and some of the obvious places to park on the north side of SH 43 (at some gated roads) are marked as no parking allowed. Quick stops at these places will allow you to scope the ponds in the refuge. Walking in the refuge area is not allowed, but much of it can be seen from the side of the road. At the eastern edge of the refuge is a dirt road called Pipeline Road; you can stop here, park, and look over part of the refuge.

Just before you reach the bridges and causeway to cross the lake, there is a good parking area on the north side of the road. This area, called Highway 43 Public Fishing Pier, provides good views over the lake and some marshy areas on the shore. There are unofficial places to park on portions of the causeway.

*Bufflehead*

Bufflehead, ring-necked duck, mallard, pied-billed grebe, American coot, Canada goose, wood duck, great blue heron, and other species can be seen here. Sometimes, the geese will be out in the lake, where double-crested cormorant and common loon can also occasionally be seen during winter. This refuge is directly on the north side of SH 43 on the western shore of Ross Barnett Reservoir, just a short distance from where SH 43 intersects with the Natchez Trace.

## VICKSBURG NATIONAL MILITARY PARK

Situated on the northern and eastern edges of Vicksburg, this unit of the National Park System presents good birding opportunities with a full dose of American history. The beautiful 1,700-acre park sits on the rolling loess hills overlooking the Mississippi River. Loess is windblown dust that was deposited in a long line through the state of Mississippi several thousand years ago, and enough accumulated to form a series of hills through the state. Part of the southern end of this loess deposit is in Vicksburg, and these hills are where the Union forces under General Grant laid siege to the Confederate forces on the hills and in the city.

The park is beautifully maintained and has virtually endless amounts of edge habitat between grassy fields and hardwood forests and brush. A long, interpretive drive through the park gives one access to the entire area. A number of sparrows are winter residents here, including savannah, fox, vesper, white-throated, white-crowned, swamp, and song sparrows. Along the river portion of the park, wintering waterfowl can sometimes be seen; these include Canada goose, greater white-fronted goose, gadwall, mallard, American wigeon, northern shoveler, lesser scaup, hooded merganser, ruddy duck, and green-winged teal. Spring migration and early summer bring as many as 34 species of warblers and vireos to the park. Mississippi kite is present in summer.

The entrance to this national park is well-marked. Take exit 4B off I-20; go north, and turn right at the first traffic light into the park. A bird list, a map, and other information about the park can be obtained by writing National Park Service, Vicksburg National Military Park, 3201 Clay Street, Vicksburg, MS 39180.

## YAZOO NATIONAL WILDLIFE REFUGE COMPLEX

Made up of five national wildlife refuges under the central management of the Yazoo National Wildlife Refuge, this complex of federal land is prime wintering waterfowl habitat along the Mississippi flyway. These refuges offer some excellent winter birding for ducks, geese, and other waterfowl. However, some of the refuges are more accessible to the birder than the others. Yazoo National Wildlife Refuge is the premier one for birders, and if you can visit only one of these five refuges, make it Yazoo. Panther Swamp National Wildlife Refuge would be the second choice for the birder, and the other three are smaller and more difficult to bird. Located in the midst of these refuges is Delta National Forest. Along with Delta National Forest, these refuges protect some of the last remaining wetlands in this vital area, as so much has been converted into farmland. Although some summer birding is possible in these areas, particularly in the national forest, winter is when these areas really stand out for birding.

Maps of the refuges and a bird list (with 250 species) for the entire complex can be obtained by writing U.S. Fish and Wildlife Service, Yazoo National Wildlife Refuge Complex, Route 1, Box 286, Hollandale, MS 38748.

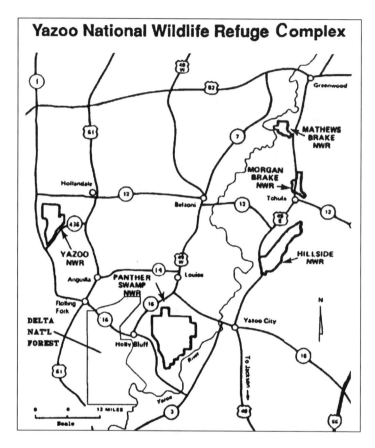

A map and information about Delta National Forest can be obtained by writing Forest Supervisor, National Forests in Mississippi, 100 W. Capitol Street, Suite 1141, Jackson, MS 39269.

## Yazoo National Wildlife Refuge

From US 61, there are two routes to Yazoo National Wildlife Refuge. From the north, take SH 436; the refuge is only about 5 miles; turn right onto Washington County

Road 34 in Bear Garden, then go left on Washington County Road 97 to reach the headquarters. From the south, take SH 14 west from Rolling Fork, and then go north on SH 1 where it intersects SH 14. On SH 1, an entrance sign points you to the right (east) into the refuge after 10.7 miles from SH 14. This entrance road is Washington County Road 97, and it will take you straight to the headquarters.

Some of the fields along the south side of this entrance road will be flooded, and sometimes, hundreds of ducks gather there. Gadwall, northern shoveler, redhead, American wigeon, American coot, and various wading birds can be seen in these flooded fields. Bring your spotting scope for good views of the waterfowl.

The center of the refuge is closed to vehicular traffic and to visitors during January and February to protect the ducks and geese, and a small area of the refuge around the headquarters is permanently closed. However, when the central portion is not closed, it is a bonanza of birds. Deer Lake is the largest lake in the middle of the central part of the refuge, and Canada goose, northern shoveler, gadwall, blue-winged teal, bufflehead, ring-necked duck, American coot, common goldeneye, green-winged teal, ruddy duck, lesser scaup, northern pintail, mallard, and sora (in early spring) may be found at Deer Lake. Near Deer Lake is the much smaller Goose Pond, which lives up to its name; Canada goose and occasionally snow goose and greater white-fronted goose can be found there. Tundra swan has also been an infrequent visitor to Yazoo. Other unusual waterfowl species that have been seen during winter and early spring at Yazoo include fulvous whistling duck, black-bellied whistling duck, cinnamon teal, oldsquaw, surf scoter, and white-winged scoter.

West of these two lakes, Alligator Pond is another good birding spot, but true to its name, this lake has a number of

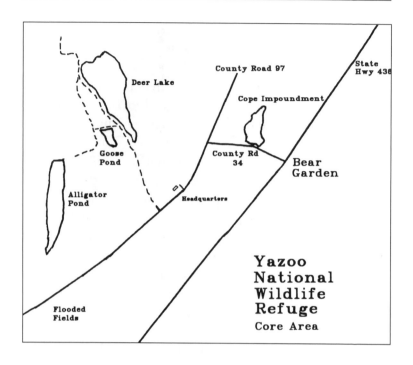

large alligators in it. Walk along the dam and look out over the shallow lake, but be careful, many of the 'gators sun and nap in the grasses along the lakeside edge of the dam. Normally, they will escape into the water with a loud splash once you get too close for their comfort; this sound can be startling. Also, the mud here can be thick and difficult to walk through. Nonetheless, Alligator Lake is worth checking out for purple gallinule, common moorhen, wood duck, and the other various duck species.

Watch for red-tailed hawk, American kestrel, and northern harrier in the field portions of the refuge. Cope Impoundment is right on County Road 34 near the Bear Garden entrance to the refuge. Check out that swampy pond for waterfowl as well.

*Purple Gallinule*

## Panther Swamp National Wildlife Refuge

Located west of Yazoo City, Panther Swamp National Wildlife Refuge is mostly inaccessible unless one is willing to walk great distances. However, two good dirt roads run along the levees on either side of the Lower Auxiliary Channel, which runs through the middle of the refuge. This refuge is run by the Fish and Wildlife Service in an area that is part of a Corps of Engineers flood control project. The two levee roads give access to and overlooks of hardwood bottomlands, swamps, fields, and flooded fields. The easiest way to reach these levee roads is to take US 49W west from Yazoo City; a sign points south to the refuge, and this is East Levee Road, but the road name is not marked. A hunter's permit station and sign mark the beginning of the refuge.

When birding along the roads here in the winter or very early spring, watch for great blue heron, eastern meadowlark, loggerhead shrike, red-tailed hawk, northern harrier, American kestrel, killdeer, great egret, and wood duck. Small ponds and flooded fields below the levee will often yield ducks, sometimes in large numbers. Waterfowl that can be seen here regularly include ring-necked duck, blue-winged teal, American coot, pied-billed grebe, gadwall, green-winged teal, northern shoveler, American wigeon, ruddy duck, canvasback, and redhead. A spotting scope will be very handy.

East Levee Road comes out onto a paved road that heads right (west) to Holly Bluff; this road crosses the channel, and the West Levee Road (also dirt) heads north back into the refuge. In the flooded fields on the west side of this road, I have seen gatherings of great egrets in the hundreds. From West Levee Road to SH 16 in Holly Bluff is 6 miles.

### Delta National Forest

Just west of Panther Swamp National Wildlife Refuge is Delta National Forest, the only bottomland hardwood national forest in the national forest system. Coming out of

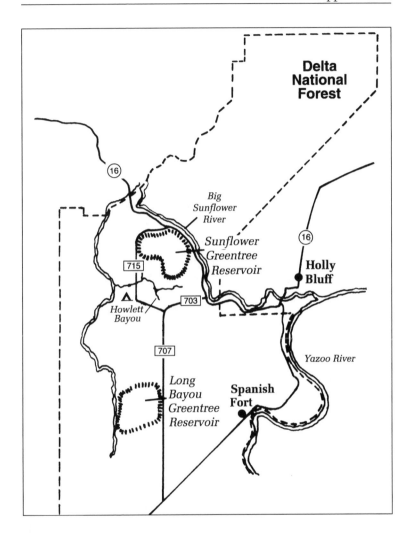

Holly Bluff, SH 16 is heading south. Just after the bridge over Big Sunflower River, barely south of Holly Bluff on SH 16, a paved road veers to the left (toward Spanish Fort) just before SH 16 makes a bend to the right (west). The Forest Service map shows this road as going straight south from the bend in SH 16, but, in fact, this road cuts off to the left from SH 16 just before SH 16 makes the bend to the west. Following this road will take you into the middle of the national forest. After about 5 miles, the road turns to dirt, but it is smooth and passable. Many of the roads in the national forest are dirt. Most are good roads, but after heavy rains they can be difficult for cars, and there are some places where the roads get washed out and are passable only to four-wheel-drive vehicles.

Taking Forest Road 707 north from the Spanish Fort road off SH 16 will bring you past the Long Bayou Greentree Reservoir. FR 707 connects at its northern end with Forest Road 703, which goes east just over 1.5 miles to SH 16, about 3 miles west of Holly Bluff. From the junction of FR 707 and FR 703, Forest Road 715 proceeds west and later turns north to Blue Lake, a very small camping area on Howlett Bayou. Blue Lake is a good place to look for wood ducks and for warblers in the spring. Listen for barred owls; they seem common here, and I have seen one cross the road in the daytime. FR 715 north of Blue Lake connects with SH 16 about 3 miles northwest of where FR 703 connects with SH 16, but during the early part of 1992, Howlett Bayou had washed out FR 715 such that only four-wheel-drive vehicles could get through that way. A sign on SH 16 indicates the direction to Blue Lake down Forest Road 703.

Much of the forest is wet, swampy hardwood forest: ideal for wood ducks. Spring and early summer bring swamp warblers here; prothonotary warbler, hooded warbler, yellow-throated warbler, and American redstart can all be heard and seen in various areas of the forest. The Long Bayou Greentree Reservoir and the Sunflower Greentree Reservoir are two good areas for waterfowl in winter; however, watching

*Prothonotary Warbler*

the waterfowl is another matter, as these are flooded hardwood areas. The trees make long-distance vision impossible.
One can walk along the levees that form these flooded
woodlands and watch for birds from them. Be careful during hunting season, as this national forest is really geared
toward that use of the bird wildlife. Sunflower Greentree
Reservoir is right on SH 16 between Forest Roads 703 and
715; it is marked, and there are two parking areas. Across the
highway from the reservoir is the Big Sunflower River, and
this area represents the most accessible birding spots in
Delta National Forest. SH 16 continues west to the town of
Rolling Fork.

## Hillside National Wildlife Refuge

Except via a dirt road along the top of a levee along the northern and western side, access to this refuge is rather difficult. Go north on US 49E from Yazoo City. After going through Eden and crossing the Yazoo County/Holmes County line, go about 2 miles and turn right (east) immediately before the highway crosses the railroad tracks; a sign points the way into the refuge. This levee road is called South Levee Road. It goes east for 2 miles and then runs northeast for the rest of the length of the refuge. The trailhead for the Alligator Slough Nature Trail is 1.5 miles down the levee road. This trail is a good place to look for wintering waterfowl and wood ducks and for prothonotary and hooded warblers in the spring. On the right side of the levee road is the refuge, and most of it is hardwood swamps that provide no major views of waterfowl areas. Once the levee road crosses Thornton Road, it becomes North Levee Road and continues on to the very northern end of the refuge; the views are much like those in the southern portion. A drive east on Thornton Road will take you through some swamps and over some of the roughest paved road around. At an intersection with a dirt road (called Hill Road) before Thornton Road goes up a hill, the refuge ends. The dirt road to the north is marked only by a sign that reads "Travel at own risk." A short trip to the north on this dirt road will take you to a large field on the west side of the road where red-tailed hawk, northern harrier, American kestrel, and wild turkey can be fairly regularly seen. DO NOT travel any further north on this unmarked road, as it is severely damaged and washed out further ahead. Getting stranded on this road will ruin your birding outing, to say the least. The North Levee Road ends at a paved road; turn left and after a mile that road will reach SH 12. From there it is 1.5 miles to the west (left) on SH 12 to its intersection with US 49E in Tchula.

Hillside National Wildlife Refuge may be good habitat for the waterfowl and for birds such as great blue heron, but it is rather difficult for the birder to get good access to these birds. The area is also extensively hunted.

## Morgan Brake National Wildlife Refuge

Small at 1,410 acres, Morgan Brake National Wildlife Refuge is split into two units. One unit lies right along US 49E, north of the town of Tchula. There are no roads or designated trails into the refuge, but a bit of bushwhacking will get you into the swampy hardwood wetlands where the wintering birds are. With the much easier access to waterfowl at Yazoo and Panther Swamp, you may not want to fight your way into Morgan Brake.

There is an information kiosk and hunting permit station at the northern end of the refuge. Up to 50,000 migratory waterfowl winter here, according to the sign; these birds include mallard, green-winged teal, gadwall, wigeon, and wood duck. Bald eagles have been sighted at the refuge. The woods in this northern area of the refuge can be hiked through. This kiosk is 5.3 miles north of the highway intersection in Tchula.

## Mathews Brake National Wildlife Refuge

Like Morgan Brake, this refuge is difficult for the birder to access. Mathews Brake is a very small refuge consisting mostly of a shallow lake with cypress and tupelo trees. It is heavily used by local fishermen, and renting a boat is about the only way to get into the refuge; standing at the boat ramp will not reveal much in the way of birds.

To reach the refuge, follow the signs from Sidon. Go west from US 49E at a triangle intersection; Melvin's One-Stop Center is in the middle of the triangle. Turn left onto School Street; then go south, west, then south again, and then the road turns west yet again. This is LeFlore County Road 511. Take a left turn, south, onto County Road 250; at the fork, take the righthand fork onto County Road 249 (there is a sign for the refuge). Drive past fields until you reach the woods on the right side of the road, and from where the woods start, everything on the right side of the road is part of the refuge. The boat ramp is ahead on the right. It is a pretty lake and cypress swamp, but a boat is necessary to explore it.

## NOXUBEE NATIONAL WILDLIFE REFUGE

About 20 miles south of Starkville lies the 47,000-acre Noxubee National Wildlife Refuge; here is the best opportunity for seeing red-cockaded woodpeckers in the states of Mississippi and Alabama, and perhaps anywhere in the South. If coming from Starkville, get on SH 25 and head south; just past the campus of Mississippi State University there will be a sign pointing the way to Noxubee. Turn left (south) onto paved Oktoc Road. Follow the signs to Noxubee at a fork in the road. After 17 miles or so, just before Oktoc Road dead-ends, it will become a dirt road. At the intersection where Oktoc Road dead-ends, turn right, or west, onto Bluff Lake Road, and drive to the main area of the refuge. Bluff Lake Road is dirt and crosses a number of one-lane bridges; the road is passable by any car, but take your time, particularly when rain has made the road muddy and slippery. After

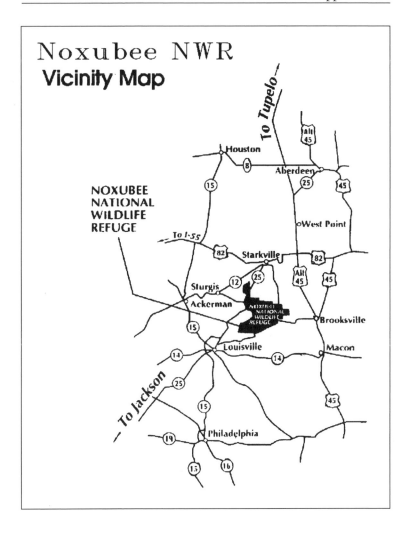

# Noxubee NWR
## Vicinity Map

To Tupelo

Alt 45

Houston

8

Aberdeen

15

NOXUBEE
NATIONAL
WILDLIFE
REFUGE

25

45

West Point

To I-55

82

Starkville

82

Sturgis

12

25

Alt 45

45

Ackerman

NOXUBEE
NATIONAL
WILDLIFE
REFUGE

Brooksville

15

Louisville

Macon

14

14

To Jackson

25

15

45

19

Philadelphia

15

16

entering the refuge, the road passes a number of swampy areas with wood duck houses in them. After crossing the Noxubee River, the road reaches Bluff Lake and goes along the dam that forms the lake, which covers approximately 1,200 acres. Bluff Lake and Loakfoma Lake, which is just south of

Bluff Lake, form the core area of about 3,225 acres where hunting is not allowed; this area around these two lakes provides the main birding territory on the refuge. After crossing the dam, the road going straight leads to Loakfoma Lake; the road to the right leads to an area between the two lakes and on to the refuge headquarters.

To reach the refuge from SH 25, south of Starkville and north of Louisville, watch for signs pointing to the east; the refuge is about 25 miles from the highway down a road that alternates between pavement and dirt, but is mostly dirt. This road is known as the Louisville Road and it passes through the tiny community of Betheden.

Stop at the headquarters and ask the rangers about current birding conditions and hot spots. Winter is the time when hundreds, and even thousands, of ducks and Canada geese winter at the refuge, primarily on Loakfoma and Bluff lakes. Bald eagles and osprey will also use the lakes during winter. During some winters, white-fronted geese and tundra swans have been seen among the Canada geese. Just before the headquarters is a small parking area. From this point, a short boardwalk takes you to an overlook where geese can be seen on part of Bluff Lake and an adjacent field. On the other side of the road is the beginning of the woodpecker trail. This short trail through an old growth pine forest provides what is in my opinion the best opportunity for sighting red-cockaded woodpeckers in the world. The trail passes by approximately two dozen nesting trees for this endangered bird, and I have never been on this trail without seeing at least two of the woodpeckers. These cavity trees are marked with white bands of paint. Listen for the distinctive "zhilp" call of the woodpecker and follow it. Every other species of woodpecker found in the South can also be seen here, so this trail provides the chance to see eight woodpecker species in one

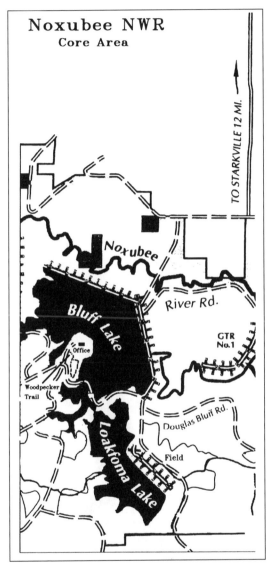

Noxubee NWR
Core Area

TO STARKVILLE 12 MI.

Noxubee

River Rd.

Bluff Lake

Office

GTR No.1

Woodpecker Trail

Douglas Bluff Rd.

Loakfoma Lake

Field

outing. Of course, the yellow-bellied sapsucker is present only during the winter, but the main attraction, the red-cockaded, is a year-round resident of this forest. I judge the odds of seeing the red-cockaded here as extremely good, and it is unlikely that you will go away from Noxubee without having seen one.

When looking for wintering ducks, I have found Loakfoma Lake more productive. Hundreds of mallards are possible; also, look for ring-necked duck, green-winged teal, northern shoveler, blue-winged teal, pied-billed grebe, canvasback, hooded merganser, American wigeon, lesser scaup, and ruddy duck. Wood ducks are fairly common in swampy areas. Rarer waterfowl that have been sighted on Noxubee include fulvous whistling duck, snow goose, American black duck, oldsquaw, common goldeneye, and surf scoter. Other unique birds that have been spotted here include anhinga, white ibis, wood stork, horned grebe, eared grebe, short-eared owl, and red crossbill.

The pine woods are filled with pine warblers, and in winter, yellow-rumped warblers are common and orange-

*Wood Stork*

crowned warblers are present. During spring and fall, Noxubee can provide good viewing of migrant species such as warblers, orioles, and vireos. Although winter is the time to see most ducks and any eagles, the other seasons at Noxubee can provide good birding experiences. The red-cockaded woodpecker is a permanent resident. Spring brings nesting black vultures, red-shouldered hawks, and wood ducks. Early summer provides nesting wild turkeys, mourning doves, eastern bluebirds, prothonotary warblers, and bob-white quail. Mid to late summer brings the first southward migrants such as cormorants, shorebirds, certain ducks, broad-winged hawks, and possibly wood storks. Autumn begins the buildup of wintering species of ducks, geese, eagles, ospreys, and woodcocks. Fish crow has also been known to winter here.

A bird list containing 254 species and indications of the relative abundance of each one during each season is available from the refuge headquarters; also available is a brochure with a detailed map of the refuge. This brochure will describe the various wildlife events that occur during the various months of the year. Contact Noxubee Refuge Manager, Route 1, Box 142, Brooksville, MS 39739.

The unit of Tombigbee National Forest on the western side of Noxubee National Wildlife Refuge is unfortunately used mostly for timber and offers few good birding opportunities. The camping and recreation area at Choctaw Lake, off SH 15 south of Ackerman, offers the best chance for birds in this small unit of the national forest system.

# Chapter 7
# Northern Mississippi

## CORPS OF ENGINEERS LAKES ALONG I-55

Strung along I-55 like a set of jewels on a necklace, four large lakes constructed by the U.S. Army Corps of Engineers for flood control and recreation provide the finest birding in northern Mississippi. Included with these lakes are swamps, marshes, miles of shoreline habitat, and three state parks. From north to south, these lakes are Arkabutla Lake, Sardis Lake, Enid Lake, and Grenada Lake. In winter, the lakes attract thousands of ducks and geese, and rare accidental species often stop here. During spring migration, these lakes provide great grassy shorelines for passing shorebirds such as sandpipers. In summer, the swamps near some of the lakes are filled with warblers and other songbirds. Fall migration finds many shorebird species returning, and numerous gulls. Recreational and camping facilities at all of these lakes are first-rate, as these lakes are major showcases for the Corps of Engineers.

Brochures are available that describe each lake and give good maps of the lakes overall and of the dam areas in particular.

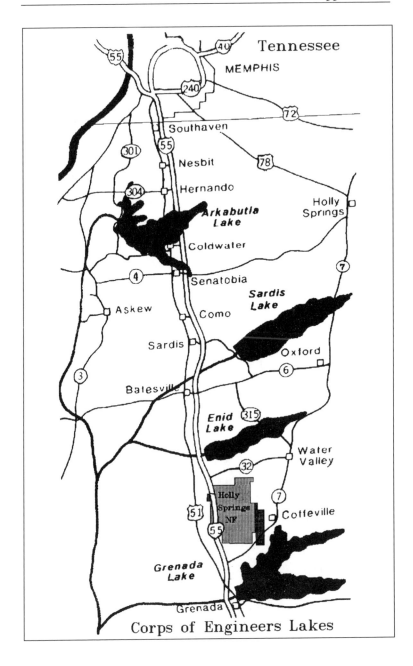

Corps of Engineers Lakes

During spring migration, the amount of habitat suitable for passing shorebirds varies from year to year with the amount of spring rain. The usual conditions in spring tend to lower the lakes and result in large areas of open, often grass-covered flats near the dams and at places along the shoreline. At this time, one can see such migrants as greater yellowlegs, lesser yellowlegs, lesser golden plover, short-billed dowitcher, whimbrel, marbled godwit, Baird's sandpiper, solitary sandpiper, spotted sandpiper, and least sandpiper. Spring migration can also include varieties of warblers and vireos, bobolink, merlin, and scarlet tanager. Autumn can include some of those species and also buff-breasted sandpiper.

A spotting scope is necessary to cover the great expanse of shorelines visible from overlook areas.

## Arkabutla Lake

Used mainly as a flood control reservoir, Arkabutla Lake can vary from 11,240 acres at low pool to over 33,000 acres at full pool. To reach the dam area, where most of the facilities and many of the good overlooks are, take exit 280 off I-55 at Hernando; go west on DeSoto County Road 304 until it reaches County Road 301 in Eudora. (CR 304 continues on these other roads as Scenic Loop 304, and south of the dam, it will take you back to I-55 at the Coldwater exit.) Then, turn left (south) and drive until the road turns left onto Pratt Road and goes to the dam. Here, the Dub Patton recreation area and campground provide numerous views over the lake. Three hiking trails begin from the picnic area along the northern side of the outlet channel. There are a short nature trail along the channel, a 2 mile loop trail, and a 5 mile loop going off the 2 mile trail. On the south side of the outlet channel is the beaver pond nature trail, which gives a short hike into the woods and swampy areas there. These trails provide good access to the woodlands below the dam. On the southern end of the dam, the South Abutment day-use area and campground and the Bayou Point picnic area provide good views over the lake. During winter, watch the lake around the dam for various gull species, ducks, and common loon. Watch for eastern bluebird in the grassy areas around the dam.

## Sardis Lake

Either because of its good location or because it is extensively birded by local birders, Sardis Lake reveals a high number of accidentals and unusual bird species for the area. Providing flood control on the Little Tallahatchie River, the coverage of the lake can fluctuate from 9,800 acres to 58,500 acres. The area around the dam and John W. Kyle State Park on the lake just north of the dam give good overviews of the lake. During winter, the lake above the dam and Lower Lake (a second, 350-acre lake below the dam) are habitat for migrating gulls, including six rare or casual species that have been spotted here. These are the Bonaparte's, little, black-headed, ring-billed, and lesser black-backed gulls, and black-legged kittiwake. Franklin's gull can sometimes be found during migration. Common loon, various duck species, and horned grebe can also be found near the dam in early winter. As many as 18 duck species have been seen regularly at this lake. During summer, Mississippi kite has nested in the dam area.

To reach the dam area and the state park from I-55, take exit 252 at Sardis and go east on SH 315, which goes right to the dam. The left fork will take you to the state park and

*Franklin's Gull*

to the road that runs along the top of the dam; the right fork goes to the camping area and to Lower Lake. The two forks rejoin, and SH 315 goes on south to intersect SH 6, which goes east to Oxford.

John W. Kyle State Park has a number of places to sit and look out over the lake and the dam. Apparently, a few of the thousands of Canada geese that winter at Sardis Lake have decided it is a nice place to stay year-round. In spring, you can spot pairs of geese walking and swimming their newly hatched goslings in the area just below the lodge, which is built on a peninsula from which you can see great views of the dam. The park has picnic areas, cabins, a boat ramp, and a short nature trail at this portion. A campground on Corps land below the dam is run as the campground for the state park.

The dam itself has good vantage points for scanning the lake at both ends, and below the dam, between it and Lower Lake, is a maze of campgrounds, picnic areas, and day-use areas. A nature/fitness trail is provided at the southern end of Lower Lake. Lower Lake is worth checking for gulls and waterfowl during winter, and many areas provide views of the lake. My favorite is Cypress Point on the west side of the lake, as it is usually less crowded and less used by other visitors.

On the portion of SH 315 north of the dam, just before the road crosses the emergency spillway for the river as you head for the dam, there is a gravel road to the west; 1.1 miles down this road is the Clear Springs Nature Trail, which includes an extensive boardwalk through a lovely cypress/tupelo swamp. There is a sign on the main road indicating that this gravel road goes to the nature trail; along the road are some crop fields that sometimes host foraging waterfowl and horned larks early in the winter months. Spring and summer songbirds can be plentiful here; species found here include prothonotary warbler, yellow-throated warbler, northern parula warbler, Swainson's warbler, Louisiana waterthrush, yellow-throated vireo, white-breasted nuthatch, and acadian flycatcher. Wood ducks also live here year-round. Perhaps due to the large number of dead, standing trees in this swamp, the densest population of red-headed woodpeckers I have ever seen lives here. Late in the afternoon, they get into fights and what seems like hammering contests, and I have seen as many as 12 at one time, without turning my head. Hairy woodpecker is also common here. The trail continues a short way through the woods on the higher ground above the swamp, but the swamp is the real treasure of this spot; it is very beautiful in the light of sunset. Be prepared though; in the summer months, the insects in this swamp, like most in the South, are fierce.

Sardis Waterfowl Refuge northwest of Oxford is the winter home of thousands of Canada geese, and small numbers of snow geese and greater white-fronted geese also winter there. The refuge headquarters can be reached by taking SH

314 out of Oxford; SH 314 (Jackson Avenue, westward out of the square) goes out of the town square downtown at its northwest corner. Turn right towards College Hill, Sardis Reservoir, and the airport on Airport Road, which is well marked with signs. After 1.1 miles, just past a right turn that goes to the airport is another right that is marked with a sign for Sardis Waterfowl Refuge; this is a four-lane road. Take another right onto a dirt road after 4.9 miles; a sign indicates this turn to the refuge. This dirt road will go 3.5 miles and dead-end into the refuge; watch for northern bobwhite, eastern bluebird, and eastern kingbird in the fields alongside the road. The refuge headquarters is mostly dedicated to the study and maintenance of the refuge and not geared towards visitors. The eastern edge of the refuge can be scanned from Hurricane Landing, which can be reached either by taking the marked connecting road (Lafayette County Road 103) off SH 314 going to the refuge headquarters or by taking Lafayette County Road 108 west off SH 7 at the Abbeville exit. Hurricane Landing has a series of boat ramps with some picnic areas and camping available; depending on the water level, a series of viewpoints west into the fields and submerged woodlands of the refuge are available; bring your spotting scope. Wood ducks are regular here.

### Enid Lake

The third, and the smallest of this string of lakes, Enid Lake varies from 6,100 to 28,000 acres in size. Many of the same bird species that have been spotted at the other lakes may also show up here. A Franklin's gull was spotted here in the spring of 1992. The camping and recreation areas around the dam are very convenient to I-55. Exit 233 will provide immediate access to the dam area where there are picnic spots, campgrounds, and a number of areas for watching birds near the dam and out over the lake.

George Payne Cossar State Park is located on the southern side of the lake, about a mile above the dam. This park has mixed pine/hardwood forests typical of the area and provides good views over part of the lake. It is reached from SH 32; take exit 227 off I-55. After about 2.5 miles, a turn to the north takes you to the park; from SH 32, it is 1.75 miles to the park entrance. The park does have a 2.5-mile nature trail through the woods; the trail begins near the boat ramp.

## Holly Springs National Forest: Yalobusha Unit

Located just off I-55 between Enid and Grenada lakes, the Yalobusha Unit of Holly Springs National Forest is a small area of fragmented, federal land. The only good spot for birders is at Lake Tillatoba, which is a 65-acre fishing lake that provides habitat for many of the typical woodland bird species of this area. These include pine warbler, brown-headed nuthatch, red-eyed vireo, white-eyed vireo, and hermit thrush, in winter. The lake is reached by taking exit 220 (Tillatoba) off I-55 onto SH 330 (if you have the Forest Service map of this area, it has 330 *incorrectly* marked); go east on SH 330 toward Coffeeville 3 miles, and the lake will be visible on the north side of the road. There are some primitive camping spots available, and the fishing is reported to be good, but its location right on a main road keeps Lake Tillatoba from being a quiet place.

## Grenada Lake

The last of the four flood-control lakes, Grenada is probably the second-best birding bet after Sardis Lake. Immediately below the dam is a managed waterfowl refuge which provides a winter home for thousands of ducks. Also, like Sardis, early winter has brought rare gulls to this lake; little gull, lesser black-backed gull, and Franklin's gull have been spotted here. Forster's terns also use this lake on their fall migration back to the Gulf coast; some of these tern migrants can show up as early as July. In winter, American tree sparrows have been sighted in this area.

The best way to reach the dam area on Grenada Lake is to take exit 206 from I-55 (the exit for SH 8); go through the town of Grenada, and then turn left at a fork onto SH 333 (scenic route) after 4.5 miles from the interstate; that road makes another left turn after 0.6 mile and takes you to the southern end of the dam. There are numerous overlooks among the recreational facilities at the southern end of the dam. A short nature trail called Old River Trail goes through the woods at this end of the dam along part of the old course of the Yalobusha River channel; this is a good spot for spring and summer warblers and other woodland songbirds. Below the dam is a small lake that is used for fishing; ducks and other waterfowl may be seen here in winter. This lake is reached from the Toe Road (the road at the bottom of the dam) by two gravel roads that take you to either the north or south side of it. Just beyond the road that takes you to the north side of that small lake is an unmarked dirt road (a sign says "No Hunting, Safety Zone") that leads to a small parking area not 200 feet from the Toe Road. Going past a gate in the road and through no more than 100 feet of woods, you come to the impounded areas where so many ducks winter. Be careful not to spook the ducks when you approach, and you will have good, close sightings of them. There are a number of other small lakes and wet areas north of these waterfowl impoundments in what is called a quail management demonstration area. Watch for northern bobwhite, purple martin, and eastern bluebird in the grassy areas and woodland edges along the bottom of the dam.

Hugh White State Park is on the southern side of Grenada Lake. It is reached from SH 8 by turning north onto a road 2.65 miles past the fork intersection of SH 8 and Scenic SH 333; 2.5 miles down this road is the entrance to the park. The park has lodging, camping, and numerous views over a portion of the lake.

In early winter or during spring migration, these four lakes and their various bird habitats can keep one busy for many days just covering the most common and accessible areas to bird. For those times of year, these lakes are highly recommended stops, and during other times, they are still pleasant places to visit. For detailed maps and brochures on these four Corps of Engineers lakes, write Sardis Lake Field Office, P.O. Drawer 186, Sardis, MS 38666.

## Grenada Waterfowl Management Area

Upriver from Grenada Lake is a state refuge for thousands of wintering waterfowl. A sign on the northern side of SH 8, 14.8 miles from the road going to Hugh White State Park, marks the refuge. This area is designed for managing the ducks and for hunting purposes, and birding it is difficult for all except local people who are familiar with the hunting seasons and the primitive roads through the area. Parking is extremely limited at this sign.

## TRACE STATE PARK

Located approximately 9 miles west of the Natchez Trace where it passes through Tupelo, Trace State Park is reached by turning north off SH 6 onto Pontotoc County Road 65, which leads straight into the park. This park covers 2,500 acres, with 600 acres in a lake that is known for its excellent bass fishing. Camping and cabins are available. Although Trace State Park has twenty miles of trail, much of that is used by ATVs, mountain bikers, and horseback riders; thus, hiking and bird watching may be interrupted regularly.

Containing an unusual geologic ridge that forms a high place in otherwise lower rolling hills, the park has a fair amount of woods and edge habitat that is attractive to migrating songbirds. Various warblers, tanagers, buntings, orioles, vireos, and other migrants are possible here, but the appearance of any particular species and its timing are random throughout the season. During the winter, various duck species sometimes use the lake. While not known as a birding hotspot, Trace State Park is a nice place and has potential for good birding.

Information about the park can be obtained by writing Trace State Park, Rt. 1, Box 254, Belden, MS 38826.

## TOMBIGBEE STATE PARK

Located off SH 6 east of the Natchez Trace where it passes through Tupelo, Tombigbee State Park is reached by going through the town of Tupelo on SH 6. About 1 mile east of the Natchez Trace, SH 6 passes the Tupelo National Battlefield Site on the right; this unit of the national park system must be one of the smallest as it barely covers three lots in the middle of town. There is no special birding at the battlefield, but it is an interesting stop for the Civil War history buff. At the eastern end of town, SH 6 turns to the south (right); if you turn left or north at this intersection, you will come to the birthplace of Elvis Presley within two blocks. After 3.2 miles on SH 6 south from the intersection, turn left onto State Park Road to get to the park. This road goes straight into the park.

There is a large lake just inside the park entrance; belted kingfisher and eastern bluebirds are often seen along the road next to the lake. Camping and cabins are available. Tree Trunk Trail takes you through a hardwood forest; the trailhead is at the road loop just past the improved campground. This is a good place to watch for various woodpecker species and for woodland songbirds such as wood thrush, yellow-throated vireo, black-and-white warbler, and summer tanager.

More information is available from Tombigbee State Park, Rt. 2, Box 336-E, Tupelo, MS 38801.

## HOLLY SPRINGS NATIONAL FOREST

Holly Springs National Forest is made up of fragmented federal and private lands. Most of the area delineated as the national forest is in private ownership. With the federal lands not grouped into any one large area, there are no opportunities for wilderness recreation, for preservation of large areas of habitat, or for long trails to be built. However, the forest does have two very nice lakes for the birder to visit and explore. Chewalla Lake, at 260 acres, is the largest of the two recreation lakes; it has camping facilities complete with 42 sites and cold showers. A primitive hiking trail goes along the south and east sides of the lake, and by following this trail around or by taking a shorter, but harder, route of bush-whacking along the west side of the lake north of the boat

*Yellow-throated Warbler*

ramp, one can reach the swampy area at the lake's upper end and perhaps spot swamp warblers such as prothonotary, hooded, and northern parula. Just south of the campground, on the trail around the lake, there is an elevated platform that gives one good views out over the lake; bring a spotting scope. Wood duck is present year-round, and during winter, various other species of ducks may be spotted on the lake. The grassy marshes around the lake have king rail during the summer months. During spring and summer, the woods around the lake are good for eastern phoebe, summer tanager, great-crested flycatcher, yellow-throated warbler, red-shouldered hawk, and broad-winged hawk.

To reach Chewalla Lake, take Marshall County Road 634 north from US 78 in the community of Lake Center, a few miles east of the town of Holly Springs. Coming from the west (Holly Springs), there is sometimes no sign to mark the turn; there is usually a sign on the other side of the road marking the way to the lake for travelers coming from the east

(Hickory Flat). If you are coming from the east, note your mileage at the intersection of US 78 and SH 349 in Potts Camp; after 5.4 miles, you reach the turn to the right (north) onto Marshall County Road 634. Go three miles; turn right onto Forest Road 611, and the lake is just over a mile ahead.

Another good lake and forest area for birders to check out is the Puskus Lake area east of Oxford. Less developed than Chewalla Lake, Puskus has plenty of quiet spots and only tent camping is available; many of these camping sites have wonderful views of the sunset over the lake. This 96-acre lake is reached by taking SH 30 east from its intersection with SH 7, just outside Oxford. Go nine miles along SH 30, and the turn to Puskus Lake is on the left (north) onto Forest Road 838, which is dirt; 2.7 miles later, you will reach the lake area. The woods and open areas around the lake are good for the species typical of this area such as eastern bluebird, brown-headed nuthatch, pine warbler, yellow-throated warbler, and others. Where the road forks to go to the separate picnic and camping areas, there is a trailhead for a short nature trail; the other end of this trail is at the parking area loop at the boat ramp, near the camping area. This trail goes through the mostly pine woods on the southern side of the lake, and it has been used for compass orienteering games and courses; this trail is not heavily used or extensively maintained. Hairy woodpecker is fairly common in these woods.

The Yalobusha Unit of the forest is discussed in the section on the Corps of Engineers lakes along I-55, as that unit is between Enid Lake and Grenada Lake on the interstate.

For more information and a map of the forest, write to Forest Supervisor, National Forests in Mississippi, 100 W. Capitol Street, Suite 1141, Jackson, MS 39269.

## WALL DOXEY STATE PARK

Although it is a very small park, Wall Doxey State Park has a great deal of charm, and it is my personal favorite of all of Mississippi's state parks. Located right on SH 7 south of Holly Springs and north of Oxford, this park provides excellent access to a beautiful cypress swamp, and its small lake attracts migrating shorebirds in the spring. From the intersection of US 78 and SH 7 south of Holly Springs, it is 6.3 miles south to the entrance of Wall Doxey. After entering the park, go past the first camping area, and then turn right before the lodge/office and go down to the boat ramp on the lake. Here there are good views over the lake and into the bald cypress swamp at the upper (northern) end of the lake. The park's nature trail begins here and goes all the way around the

*Wood Thrush*

lake and back to this spot. In spring, watch the shores of the lake for migrant shorebirds such as spotted sandpiper, upland sandpiper, solitary sandpiper, and others; I have seen spotted sandpipers standing right on the dock next to the ramp during May. The nature trail will take you to a lookout tower overlooking an overgrown beaver pond north of the main lake. In the woods along the trail, prothonotary warbler and wood thrush are common and can be seen at quite close range. While on the trail, also watch for hooded warbler, yellow-throated warbler, American redstart, wood duck, Louisiana waterthrush, and other woodland and swamp species.

The park has campgrounds and cabins. Information about the park can be obtained by writing Wall Doxey State Park, Holly Springs, MS 38635.

## J. P. COLEMAN STATE PARK

With numerous expansive views over Pickwick Lake on the Tennessee River, J. P. Coleman State Park, in the very northeastern corner of Mississippi, is a good spot for watching wintering waterfowl. Complete with a marina, lodge, restaurant, cabins, and a campground, this park provides nice accommodations on a large lake. Views out over the water can be had almost anywhere in the park, but my favorite spot for watching for wintering waterfowl and common loons is the picnic pavilion on an arm of land that juts out into the lake between the office and the primitive campground. The park also has a nature trail through the woods from the ranger station on the entrance road to the first picnic pavilion. There are also nature preserve areas south of the developed, family campground and across the Indian Creek portion of the lake; these two areas are more difficult to reach. The one south of the campground can be reached by walking through the campground and then heading on into the woods; a boat is needed to reach the area across Indian Creek. During spring and summer, species normally seen in this area such as white-breasted nuthatch, indigo bunting, summer tanager, Acadian flycatcher, various woodpeckers, eastern pewee, and yellow-throated warbler are present, and during migration seasons, migrant songbirds can be found in these areas, with some luck.

To reach the park, take SH 25 north from US 72, near Iuka. SH 25 will make its way through Iuka; after 5.2 miles, a well-marked road to the right, Tishomingo County Road 989, leads to the state park. Turn right at an intersection after 6.5 miles onto Tishomingo County Road 321; this paved road will ford a small stream and go straight into J. P. Coleman State Park.

Information about the park can be obtained by writing J. P. Coleman State Park, Rt. 5, Box 504, Iuka, MS 38852.

# Chapter 8
# Hot Birds

This is a listing of the rarer species possible in Alabama and Mississippi, and those birds that are found only in the South; included in this list are the locations in these two states that are the best spots to try to see these birds. This list is a rather subjective register of birds that one would most want to spot on any trip to the deep South, and it is in no way a complete listing of the areas where these birds may be sighted. This list covers those areas discussed in this book.

## Red-cockaded Woodpecker

Perhaps the rarest and most sought after bird resident year-round in the southern states is the red-cockaded woodpecker. This is one of the premier birds to sight if visiting in Alabama and Mississippi. Without doubt, the best chance of spotting one is in Noxubee National Wildlife Refuge in Mississippi. If you need this species for your life list and have only one shot at finding it, go to Noxubee. The most easily accessible spot from a major interstate highway is at the Bienville Pines Scenic Area in Bienville National Forest, Mississippi. The best chance for seeing many of the birds in a relatively large expanse of their natural habitat is in the Oakmulgee District of the Talladega National Forest in Alabama, and there is a good place just off Alabama SH 25 in the Oakmulgee. Also, in the Conecuh National Forest in Alabama, there is one good viewing location that is easy to find. The woodpeckers also can be found in Gulf State Park, Alabama, in DeSoto National Forest, Mississippi, and in other areas, but the chances of actually seeing the birds in those places are low.

## Anhinga

Choctaw National Wildlife Refuge, Alabama; Bon Secour National Wildlife Refuge, Alabama.

## Sandhill Crane

The Mississippi subspecies can best be sighted at Mississippi Sandhill Crane National Wildlife Refuge. Other, but less probable, places to see the cranes are at Eufaula National Wildlife Refuge in Alabama and Gulf State Park, Alabama, during February.

## Magnificent Frigatebird

During summer months, this bird may be seen offshore of both states. A boat trip may be necessary, or storms may bring one close to the beaches.

## Wood Stork

Rare at Bon Secour National Wildlife Refuge, Alabama; Choctaw National Wildlife Refuge, Alabama; and Noxubee National Wildlife Refuge, Mississippi.

*Sandhill Crane*

## Fulvous Whistling Duck

On rare occasions, this bird has been seen during winter at Noxubee National Wildlife Refuge in Mississippi and at Wheeler National Wildlife Refuge in Alabama.

## White-fronted Goose

During winter, try looking among the Canada geese at Noxubee National Wildlife Refuge in Mississippi.

## Swallow-tailed Kite

Seen occasionally at Dauphin Island, Alabama; Choctaw National Wildlife Refuge, Alabama; Bon Secour National Wildlife Refuge, Alabama; Historic Blakeley State Park,

Alabama; and along the Mississippi coast at Gulf Islands National Seashore.

## White-tailed Tropicbird

Dauphin Island, Alabama; Gulf Islands National Seashore; offshore from either coast.

## Masked Booby

Bon Secour National Wildlife Refuge, Alabama; Fort Morgan, Alabama; Dauphin Island, Alabama.

## Brown Booby

Bon Secour National Wildlife Refuge, Alabama; Fort Morgan, Alabama; Dauphin Island, Alabama.

## Northern Gannet

Bon Secour National Wildlife Refuge, Alabama; Fort Morgan, Alabama; Dauphin Island, Alabama; Perdido Pass, Alabama; Gulf State Park, Alabama.

## Peregrine Falcon

Dauphin Island, Alabama; Meaher State Park, Alabama; Bon Secour National Wildlife Refuge, Alabama.

## Bald Eagle

Lake Guntersville State Park, Alabama, in January. Less likely to be seen at Noxubee National Wildlife Refuge, Mississippi, and Choctaw National Wildlife Refuge, Alabama.

## Piping Plover

Beach area of Bon Secour National Wildlife Refuge, Alabama, in winter.

## Roseate Tern

During spring and fall migration, Bon Secour National Wildlife Refuge, Alabama; sightings are rare, usually only after storms have swept up the Atlantic coast.

## Least Tern

Nesting beach in Biloxi, Mississippi; beach area of Bon Secour National Wildlife Refuge, Alabama; Dauphin Island, Alabama. Fairly easily seen at any shoreline area in these two states.

## Burrowing Owl

Fort at East Ship Island, Gulf Islands National Seashore, Mississippi; beaches at Dauphin Island and Bon Secour National Wildlife Refuge, Alabama.

## Groove-billed Ani

Gulf Islands National Seashore in Mississippi; Dauphin Island and Bon Secour National Wildlife Refuge, Alabama.

## Red-throated Loon

Dauphin Island, Alabama, in winter and early spring; very rare.

## Mottled Duck

Blakely Island state-owned industrial area, Alabama.

## Black-necked Stilt

Blakely Island state-owned industrial area, Alabama.

## Reddish Egret

Dauphin Island, Alabama; possible at any number of coastal areas.

## Brown Pelican

Once near the brink of extinction, the brown pelican has recovered very nicely, particularly in Alabama. Almost all coastal areas will guarantee views of brown pelicans; anywhere along the Alabama beaches will provide a view of a flight of pelicans coming by. One need only wait for a little while. Very common around the docks and pilings at Fort Morgan, Alabama, and Dauphin Island, Alabama. Less common in Mississippi, but still very likely in areas with pilings and docks, such as Gulf Islands National Seashore.

# Appendix 1
# A Checklist of Alabama
# and Mississippi Birds

This Appendix is based upon the *Field Checklist of Alabama Birds* prepared by the Alabama Ornithological Society, checklists of the various parks and refuges in the two states, and confirmed sightings of species seen after the date of the AOS checklist, which is October 1991. This list contains 406 species, two of which are extinct and three of which are extirpated. The species marked hypothetical are those listed as such by the AOS; however, some species listed as hypothetical in late 1991 have since been confirmed by sightings by several experienced birders, and those species are listed here as Accidental.

The English and scientific names and sequence follow the *ABA Checklist: Birds of the Continental United States and Canada,* published by the American Birding Association (Fourth Edition, 1990).

The following symbols are used:

(X)   Extinct
(E)   Extirpated
(A)   Accidental

(H)  Hypothetical
(I)   Introduced
(En) Endangered or Threatened Species under the
       Endangered Species Act
 *     Has bred in these states

## AVES: Birds

**GAVIIFORMES: Loons**
 GAVIIDAE: Loons

Red-throated Loon (A)
 *Gavia stellata*
Arctic Loon (A)
 *G. arctica*
Pacific Loon (A)
 *G. pacifica*

Common Loon
 *G. immer*

**PODICIPEDIFORMES:
 Grebes**
PODICIPEDIDAE:
 Grebes

Pied-billed Grebe *
 *Podilymbus podiceps*

Horned Grebe
*Podiceps auritus*
Red-necked Grebe
*P. grisegena*
Eared Grebe
*P. nigricollis*
Western Grebe (A)
*Aechmophorus occidentalis*
Clark's Grebe (A)
*A. clarkii*

**PROCELLARIIFORMES: Tube-nosed Swimmers**
PROCELLARIIDAE: Shearwaters and Petrels

Cory's Shearwater (A)
*Calonectris diomedea*
Greater Shearwater (A)
*Puffinus gravis*
Sooty Shearwater (A)
*P. griseus*
Audubon's Shearwater (A)
*P. lherminieri*

HYDROBATIDAE: Storm-Petrels

Wilson's Storm-Petrel (A)
*Oceanites oceanicus*
Leach's Storm-Petrel (A)
*Oceanodroma leucorhoa*

**PELECANIFORMES: Totipalmate Swimmers**
PHAETHONTIDAE: Tropicbirds

White-tailed Tropicbird (H)
*Phaethon lepturus*

SULIDAE: Boobies and Gannets

Masked Booby (A)
*Sula dactylatra*
Brown Booby (A)
*S. leucogaster*
Northern Gannet
*Morus bassanus*

PELECANIDAE: Pelicans

American White Pelican
*Pelecanus erythrorhynchos*
Brown Pelican *
*P. occidentalis*

PHALACROCORACIDAE: Cormorants

Great Cormorant (A)
*Phalacrocorax carbo*
Double-crested Cormorant
*P. auritus*

Olivaceous Cormorant (A)
*P. brasilianus*

ANHINGIDAE: Darters

Anhinga *
*Anhinga anhinga*

FREGATIDAE:
Frigatebirds

Magnificent Frigatebird
*Fregata magnificens*

**CICONIIFORMES:
Herons, Ibises, and
Storks**
ARDEIDAE: Bitterns and
Herons

American Bittern
*Botaurus lentiginosus*
Least Bittern *
*Ixobrychus exilis*
Great Blue Heron *
*Ardea herodias*
Great Egret *
*Casmerodius albus*
Snowy Egret *
*Egretta thula*
Little Blue Heron *
*E. caerulea*

Tricolored Heron *
*E. tricolor*
Reddish Egret *
*E. rufescens*
Cattle Egret *
*Bubulcus ibis*
Green-backed Heron *
*Butorides striatus*
Black-crowned Night-
Heron *
*Nycticorax nycticorax*
Yellow-crowned Night-
heron *
*Nyctanassa violacea*

THRESKIORNITHIDAE:
Ibises and Spoonbills

White Ibis *
*Eudocimus albus*
Scarlet Ibis (H)
*E. ruber*
Glossy Ibis *
*Plegadis falcinellus*
White-faced Ibis *
*P. chihi*
Roseate Spoonbill (A)
*Ajaia ajaja*

CICONIIDAE: Storks

Wood Stork (En)
*Mycteria americana*

**ANSERIFORMES:
Swans, Geese, and
Ducks**
ANATIDAE: Swans,
Geese, and Ducks

Fulvous Whistling-
Duck *
*Dendrocygna bicolor*
Black-bellied Whistling-
Duck (A)
*D. autumnalis*
Tundra Swan (A)
*Cygnus columbianus*
Greater White-fronted
Goose
*Anser albifrons*
Snow Goose
*Chen caerulescens*
Ross' Goose (A)
*C. rossii*
Brant (A)
*Branta bernicla*
Canada Goose *
*B. canadensis*
Wood Duck *
*Aix sponsa*
Green-winged Teal
*Anas crecca*
American Black Duck *
*A. rubripes*
Mottled Duck *
*A. fulvigula*

Mallard *
*A. platyrhynchos*
White-cheeked Pintail (A)
*A. bahamensis*
Northern Pintail
*A. acuta*
Blue-winged Teal *
*A. discors*
Cinnamon Teal (A)
*A. cyanoptera*
Northern Shoveler
*A. clypeata*
Gadwall
*A. strepera*
Eurasian Wigeon (A)
*A. penelope*
American Wigeon
*A. americana*
Canvasback
*Aythya valisineria*
Redhead
*A. americana*
Ring-necked Duck
*A. collaris*
Greater Scaup
*A. marila*
Lesser Scaup
*A. affinis*
King Eider (H)
*Somateria spectabilis*
Harlequin Duck (A)
*Histrionicus histrionicus*

Oldsquaw
*Clangula hyemalis*
Black Scoter
*Melanitta nigra*
Surf Scoter
*M. perspicillata*
White-winged Scoter
*M. fusca*
Common Goldeneye
*Bucephala clangula*
Bufflehead
*B. albeola*
Hooded Merganser *
*Lophodytes cucullatus*
Common Merganser
*Mergus merganser*
Red-breasted Merganser
*M. serrator*
Ruddy Duck
*Oxyura jamaicensis*

**FALCONIFORMES:**
**Diurnal Birds of Prey**
CATHARTIDAE:
American Vultures

Black Vulture *
*Coragyps atratus*
Turkey Vulture *
*Cathartes aura*

ACCIPITRIDAE: Kites,
Hawks, Eagles, and Allies

Osprey *
*Pandion haliaetus*
American Swallow-tailed
Kite *
*Elanoides forficatus*
Black-shouldered Kite (A)
*Elanus caeruleus*
Mississippi Kite *
*Ictinia mississippiensis*
Bald Eagle (En) *
*Haliaeetus leucocephalus*
Northern Harrier
*Circus cyaneus*
Sharp-shinned Hawk *
*Accipiter striatus*
Cooper's Hawk *
*A. cooperii*
Northern Goshawk (A)
*A. gentilis*
Red-shouldered Hawk *
*Buteo lineatus*
Broad-winged Hawk *
*B. platypterus*
Swainson's Hawk (A)
*B. swainsoni*
Red-tailed Hawk *
*B. jamaicensis*
Ferruginous Hawk (H)
*B. regalis*
Rough-legged Hawk (A)
*B. lagopus*
Golden Eagle
*Aquila chysaetos*

FALCONIDAE: Caracaras and Falcons

American Kestrel *
*Falco sparverius*
Merlin
*F. columbarius*
Peregrine Falcon (En) *
*F. peregrinus*
Prairie Falcon (A)
*F. mexicanus*

**GALLIFORMES: Gallinaceous Birds**

PHASIANIDAE: Partridges, Grouse, Turkeys, and Quail

Ruffed Grouse *
*Bonasa umbellus*
Wild Turkey *
*Meleagris gallapavo*
Northern Bobwhite *
*Colinus virginianus*

**GRUIFORMES: Cranes and Rails**
RALLIDAE: Rails, Gallinules, and Coots

Yellow Rail
*Coturnicops noveboracensis*

Black Rail
*Laterallus jamaicensis*
Clapper Rail *
*Rallus longirostris*
King Rail *
*R. elegans*
Virginia Rail
*R. limicola*
Sora
*Porzana carolina*
Purple Gallinule *
*Porphyrula martinica*
Common Moorhen *
*Gallinula chloropus*
American Coot *
*Fulica americana*

GRUIDAE: Cranes

Sandhill Crane *
*Grus canadensis*
Whooping Crane (En) (H)
*G. americana*

**CHARADRIIFORMES: Shorebirds and Gulls**
CHARADRIIDAE: Plovers and Lapwings

Black-bellied Plover
*Pluvialis squatarola*
Lesser Golden-Plover
*P. domenica*

Snowy Plover *
  *Charadrius alexandrinus*
Wilson's Plover *
  *C. wilsonia*
Semipalmated Plover
  *C. semipalmatus*
Piping Plover (En)
  *C. melodus*
Killdeer *
  *C. vociferus*
Mountain Plover (A)
  *C. montanus*

HAEMATOPODIDAE:
  Oystercatchers

American Oystercatcher *
  *Haematopus palliatus*

RECURVIROSTRIDAE:
  Stilts and Avocets

Black-necked Stilt *
  *Himantopus mexicanus*
American Avocet
  *Recurvirostra ameri-
  cana*

SCOLOPACIDAE:
  Sandpipers, Phalaropes,
  and Allies

Greater Yellowlegs
  *Tringa melanoleuca*

Lesser Yellowlegs
  *T. flavipes*
Solitary Sandpiper
  *T. solitaria*
Willet *
  *Catoptrophorus semi-
  palmatus*
Spotted Sandpiper *
  *Actitis macularia*
Upland Sandpiper
  *Bartramia longicauda*
Whimbrel
  *Numenius phaeopus*
Long-billed Curlew
  *N. americanus*
Hudsonian Godwit (A)
  *Limosa haemastica*
Marbled Godwit
  *L. fedoa*
Ruddy Turnstone
  *Arenaria interpres*
Red Knot
  *Calidris canutus*
Sanderling
  *C. alba*
Semipalmated Sand-
  piper
  *C. pusilla*
Western Sandpiper
  *C. mauri*
Least Sandpiper
  *C. minutilla*

White-rumped Sandpiper
  *C. fuscicollis*
Baird's Sandpiper (A)
  *C. bairdii*
Pectoral Sandpiper
  *C. melanotos*
Sharp-tailed Sandpiper (A)
  *C. acuminata*
Dunlin
  *C. alpina*
Curlew Sandpiper (A)
  *C. ferruginea*
Stilt Sandpiper
  *C. himantopus*
Buff-breasted Sandpiper
  *Tryngites subruficollis*
Ruff (A)
  *Philomachus pugnax*
Short-billed Dowitcher
  *Limnodromus griseus*
Long-billed Dowitcher
  *L. scolopaceus*
Common Snipe
  *Gallinago gallinago*
Eurasian Woodcock (H)
  *Scolopax rusticola*
American Woodcock *
  *S. minor*
Wilson's Phalarope
  *Phalaropus tricolor*
Red-necked Phalarope (A)
  *P. lobatus*

Red Phalarope (A)
  *P. fulicaria*

LARIDAE: Skuas, Gulls, Terns, and Skimmers

Pomarine Jaeger (A)
  *Stercorarius pomarinus*
Parasitic Jaeger (A)
  *S. parasiticus*
Long-tailed Jaeger (H)
  *S. longicaudus*
Laughing Gull *
  *Larus atricilla*
Franklin's Gull (A)
  *L. pipixcan*
Little Gull (A)
  *L. minutus*
Bonaparte's Gull
  *L. philadelphia*
Ring-billed Gull
  *L. delawarensis*
Herring Gull *
  *L. argentatus*
Iceland Gull (A)
  *L. glaucoides*
Lesser Black-backed Gull (A)
  *L. fuscus*
Glaucous Gull (A)
  *L. hyperboreus*
Great Black-backed Gull (A)
  *L. marinus*

Black-legged kittiwake (A)
  *Rissa tridactyla*
Sabine's Gull (A)
  *Xema sabini*
Gull-billed Tern *
  *Sterna nilotica*
Caspian Tern *
  *S. caspia*
Royal Tern *
  *S. maxima*
Sandwich Tern *
  *S. sandvicensis*
Roseate Tern (A)
  *S. dougallii*
Common Tern *
  *S. hirundo*
Forster's Tern *
  *S. forsteri*
Least Tern (En) *
  *S. antillarum*
Bridled Tern (A)
  *S. anaethetus*
Sooty Tern (A)
  *S. fuscata*
Black Tern
  *Chlidonias niger*
Brown Noddy (A)
  *Anous stolidus*
Black Skimmer *
  *Rynchops niger*

**COLUMBIFORMES:
Pigeons and Doves**
COLUMBIDAE: Pigeons
and Doves

Rock Dove (I) *
  *Columba livia*
Band-tailed Pigeon (H)
  *C. fasciata*
Ringed Turtle-Dove (I) *
  *Streptopelia risoria*
White-winged Dove
  *Zenaida asiatica*
Mourning Dove *
  *Z. macroura*
Passenger Pigeon (X)
  *Ectopistes migratorius*
Common Ground-Dove *
  *Columbina passerina*

**PSITTACIFORMES:
Parrots**
PSITTACIDAE: Lories,
  Parakeets, Macaws, and
  Parrots

Carolina Parakeet (X)
  *Conuropsis carolinensis*

**CUCULIFORMES:
Cuckoos**
CUCULIDAE: Cuckoos,
  Roadrunners, and Anis

Black-billed Cuckoo *
*Coccyzus erythropthal-
mus*
Yellow-billed Cuckoo *
*C. americanus*
Groove-billed Ani (A)
*Crotophaga sulcirostris*

## STRIGIFORMES: Owls
TYTONIDAE: Barn Owls

Barn Owl *
*Tyto alba*

STRIGIDAE: Typical Owls

Eastern Screech-Owl *
*Otus asio*
Great Horned Owl *
*Bubo virginianus*
Snowy Owl (A)
*Nyctea scandiaca*
Burrowing Owl
*Athene cunicularia*
Barred Owl *
*Strix varia*
Long-eared Owl
*Asio otus*
Short-eared Owl
*A. flammeus*
Northern Saw-whet Owl (A)
*Aegolius acadicus*

## CAPRIMULGIFORMES: Goatsuckers
CAPRIMULGIDAE: Goat-
suckers

Lesser Nighthawk (A)
*Chordeiles acutipennis*
Common Nighthawk *
*C. minor*
Chuck-will's-widow *
*Caprimulgus caroli-
nensis*
Whip-poor-will *
*C. vociferus*

## APODIFORMES: Swifts and Hummingbirds
APODIDAE: Swifts

Chimney Swift *
*Chaetura pelagica*

TROCHILIDAE:
Hummingbirds

Buff-bellied Humming-
bird (A)
*Amazilia yucatanensis*
Ruby-throated Hum-
mingbird *
*Archilochus colubris*

Black-chinned Humming-
bird (A)
*A. alexandri*
Calliope Hummingbird
(A)
*Stellula calliope*
Rufous Hummingbird (A)
*Selasphorus rufus*
Allen's Hummingbird (A)
*S. sasin*

**CORACIIFORMES:
Kingfishers**
ALCENDINIDAE:
Kingfishers

Belted Kingfisher *
*Ceryle alcyon*

**PICIFORMES:
Woodpeckers**
PICIDAE: Woodpeckers
and Allies

Red-headed Woodpecker *
*Melanerpes erythro-
cephalus*
Red-bellied Woodpecker *
*M. carolinus*
Yellow-bellied Sapsucker
*Sphyrapicus varius*
Downy Woodpecker *
*Picoides pubescens*

Hairy Woodpecker *
*P. villosus*
Red-cockaded Wood-
pecker (En) *
*P. borealis*
Northern Flicker *
*Colaptes auratus*
Pileated Woodpecker *
*Dryocopus pileatus*
Ivory-billed Woodpecker
(E) (En) *
*Campephilis principalis*

**PASSERIFORMES:
Passerine Birds**
TYRANNIDAE: Tyrant
Flycatchers

Olive-sided Flycatcher
*Contopus borealis*
Eastern Wood-Pewee *
*C. virens*
Yellow-bellied Flycatcher
(A)
*Empidonax flaviventris*
Acadian Flycatcher *
*E. virescens*
Alder Flycatcher
*E. alnorum*
Willow Flycatcher
*E. traillii*
Least Flycatcher
*E. minimus*

Eastern Phoebe *
  *Sayornis phoebe*
Say's Phoebe (A)
  *S. saya*
Vermilion Flycatcher (A)
  *Pyrocephalus rubinus*
Ash-throated Flycatcher
  (A)
  *Myiarchus cinerascens*
Great Crested Flycatcher *
  *M. crinitus*
La Sagra's Flycatcher (A)
  *M. sagrae*
Sulphur-bellied Flycatcher
  (A)
  *Myiodynastes luteiventris*
Couch's Kingbird (A)
  *Tyrannus couchii*
Western Kingbird
  *T. verticalis*
Eastern Kingbird *
  *T. tyrannus*
Gray Kingbird *
  *T. dominicensis*
Scissor-tailed Flycatcher *
  *T. forficatus*
Fork-tailed Flycatcher (H)
  *T. savana*

ALAUDIDAE: Larks

Horned Lark *
  *Eremophila alpestris*

HIRUNDINIDAE:
Swallows

Purple Martin *
  *Progne subis*
Tree Swallow *
  *Tachycineta bicolor*
Northern Rough-winged
  Swallow *
  *Stelgidopteryx ser-
    ripennis*
Bank Swallow *
  *Riparia riparia*
Cliff Swallow *
  *Hirundo pyrrhonota*
Cave Swallow (A)
  *H. fulva*
Barn Swallow *
  *H. rustica*

CORVIDAE: Jays,
Magpies, and Crows

Blue Jay *
  *Cyanocitta cristata*
American Crow *
  *Corvus brachyrhynchos*
Fish Crow *
  *C. ossifragus*
Common Raven (E)
  *C. corax*

PARIDAE: Titmice

Carolina Chickadee *
*Parus carolinensis*
Tufted Titmouse *
*P. bicolor*

SITTIDAE: Nuthatches

Red-breasted Nuthatch
*Sitta canadensis*
White-breasted Nuthatch *
*S. carolinensis*
Brown-headed Nuthatch *
*S. pusilla*

CERTHIIDAE: Creepers

Brown Creeper
*Certhia americana*

TROGLODYTIDAE: Wrens

Rock Wren (A)
*Salpinctes obsoletus*
Carolina Wren *
*Thryothorus ludovi-
cianus*
Bewick's Wren *
*Thryomanes bewickii*
House Wren *
*Troglodytes aedon*
Winter Wren
*T. troglodytes*

Sedge Wren
*Cistothorus platensis*
Marsh Wren *
*C. palustris*

MUSCICAPIDAE: Old
World Warblers, Old
World Flycatchers,
Thrushes, and Wrentit

Golden-crowned
Kinglet
*Regulus satrapa*
Ruby-crowned Kinglet
*R. calendula*
Blue-Gray Gnatcatcher *
*Polioptila caerulea*
Northern Wheatear (A)
*Oenanthe oenanthe*
Eastern Bluebird *
*Sialia sialis*
Veery
*Catharus fuscescens*
Gray-cheeked Thrush
*C. minimus*
Swainson's Thrush
*C. ustulatus*
Hermit Thrush
*C. guttatus*
Wood Thrush *
*Hylocichla mustelina*
American Robin *
*Turdus migratorius*

Varied Thrush (A)
 *Ixoreus naevius*

MIMIDAE: Mockingbirds,
Thrashers, and Allies

Gray Catbird *
 *Dumetella carolinensis*
Northern Mockingbird *
 *Mimus polyglottos*
Sage Thrasher (A)
 *Oreoscoptes montanus*
Brown Thrasher *
 *Toxostoma rufum*

MOTACILLIDAE:
Wagtails and Pipits

Yellow Wagtail (A)
 *Motacilla flava*
American Pipit
 *Anthus rubescens*
Sprague's Pipit (A)
 *A. spragueii*

BOMBYCILLIDAE:
Waxwings

Cedar Waxwing *
 *Bombycilla cedrorum*

LANIIDAE: Shrikes

Loggerhead Shrike *
 *Lanius ludovicianus*

STURNIDAE: Starlings
and Allies

European Starling (I) *
 *Sturnus vulgaris*

VIREONIDAE: Vireos

White-eyed Vireo *
 *Vireo griseus*
Bell's Vireo (A)
 *V. bellii*
Solitary Vireo *
 *V. solitarius*
Yellow-throated Vireo *
 *V. flavifrons*
Warbling Vireo *
 *V. gilvus*
Philadelphia Vireo
 *V. philadelphicus*
Red-eyed Vireo *
 *V. olivaceus*
Black-whiskered Vireo
 *V. altiloquus*

EMBERIZIDAE: Wood-
warblers, Bananaquit,
Tanagers, Cardinals,
Grosbeaks, Emberizines,
Blackbirds, and Allies

Bachman's Warbler (En)
 (E) *
 *Vermivora bachmanii*

Blue-winged Warbler *
  *V. pinus*
Golden-winged Warbler
  *V. chrysoptera*
Tennessee Warbler
  *V. peregrina*
Orange-crowned Warbler
  *V. celata*
Nashville Warbler
  *V. ruficapilla*
Northern Parula *
  *Parula americana*
Yellow Warbler *
  *Dendroica petechia*
Chestnut-sided Warbler
  *D. pensylvanica*
Magnolia Warbler
  *D. magnolia*
Cape May Warbler
  *D. tigrina*
Black-throated Blue Warbler
  *D. caerulescens*
Yellow-rumped Warbler
  *D. coronata*
Black-throated Gray Warbler (A)
  *D. nigrescens*
Black-throated Green Warbler *
  *D. virens*
Blackburnian Warbler
  *D. fusca*

Yellow-throated Warbler *
  *D. dominica*
Pine Warbler *
  *D. pinus*
Kirtland's Warbler (En) (H)
  *D. kirtlandii*
Prairie Warbler *
  *D. discolor*
Palm Warbler
  *D. palmarum*
Bay-breasted Warbler
  *D. castanea*
Blackpoll Warbler
  *D. striata*
Cerulean Warbler *
  *D. cerulea*
Black-and-white Warbler *
  *Mniotilta varia*
American Redstart *
  *Setophaga ruticilla*
Prothonotary Warbler *
  *Protonotaria citrea*
Worm-eating Warbler *
  *Helmitheros vermivorus*
Swainson's Warbler *
  *Limnothlypis swainsonii*
Ovenbird *
  *Seiurus aurocapillus*
Northern Waterthrush
  *S. noveboracensis*
Louisiana Waterthrush *
  *S. motacilla*

Kentucky Warbler *
*Oporornis formosus*
Connecticut Warbler
*O. agilis*
Mourning Warbler
*O. philadelphia*
Common Yellow-throat *
*Geothlypis trichas*
Hooded Warbler *
*Wilsonia citrina*
Wilson's Warbler
*W. pusilla*
Canada Warbler
*W. canadensis*
Painted Redstart (H)
*Myioborus pictus*
Yellow-breasted Chat *
*Icteria virens*
Summer Tanager *
*Piranga rubra*
Scarlet Tanager *
*P. olivacea*
Western Tanager (A)
*P. ludoviciana*
Northern Cardinal *
*Cardinalis cardinalis*
Rose-breasted Grosbeak
*Pheucticus ludovi-
cianus*
Black-headed Grosbeak
(A)
*P. melanocephalus*

Blue Grosbeak *
*Guiraca caerulea*
Indigo Bunting *
*Passerina cyanea*
Painted Bunting *
*P. ciris*
Dickcissel *
*Spiza americana*
Green-tailed Towhee (A)
*Pipilo chlorurus*
Rufous-sided Towhee *
*P. erythrophthalmus*
Bachman's Sparrow *
*Aimophila aestivalis*
American Tree Sparrow
(A)
*Spizella arborea*
Chipping Sparrow *
*S. passerina*
Clay-colored Sparrow
(A)
*S. pallida*
Field Sparrow *
*S. pusilla*
Vesper Sparrow
*Pooecetes gramineus*
Lark Sparrow *
*Chondestes gramma-
cus*
Lark Bunting (A)
*Calamospiza melano-
corys*

Savannah Sparrow
*Passerculus sand-wichensis*
Grasshopper Sparrow *
*Ammodramus savan-narum*
Henslow's Sparrow
*A. henslowii*
Le Conte's Sparrow
*A. leconteii*
Sharp-tailed Sparrow
*A. caudacutus*
Seaside Sparrow *
*A. maritimus*
Fox Sparrow
*Passerella iliaca*
Song Sparrow *
*Melospiza melodia*
Lincoln's Sparrow
*M. lincolnii*
Swamp Sparrow
*M. georgiana*
White-throated Sparrow
*Zonotrichia albicollis*
White-crowned Sparrow
*Z. leucophrys*
Harris' Sparrow (A)
*Z. querula*
Dark-eyed Junco
*Junco hyemalis*
Lapland Longspur
*Calcarius lapponicus*

Smith's Longspur (A)
*C. pictus*
Bobolink
*Dolichonyx oryzivorus*
Red-winged Blackbird *
*Agelaius phoeniceus*
Eastern Meadowlark *
*Sturnella magna*
Western Meadowlark
*S. neglecta*
Yellow-headed Blackbird
*Xanthocephalus xan-thocephalus*
Rusty Blackbird
*Euphagus carolinus*
Brewer's Blackbird
*E. cyanocephalus*
Boat-tailed Grackle *
*Quiscalus major*
Common Grackle *
*Q. quiscula*
Shiny Cowbird (A)
*Molothrus bonariensis*
Bronzed Cowbird (A)
*M. aeneus*
Brown-headed Cowbird *
*M. ater*
Orchard Oriole *
*Icterus spurius*
Northern Oriole *
*I. galbula*

FRINGILLIDAE:
Fringillina and
Cardueline Finches and
Allies

Purple Finch
*Carpodacus purpureus*
House Finch *
*C. mexicanus*
Red Crossbill (A)
*Loxia curvirostra*
Common Redpoll (A)
*Carduelis flammea*

Pine Siskin
*C. pinus*
American Goldfinch *
*C. tristis*
Evening Grosbeak
*Coccothraustes vesper-
tinus*

PASSERIDAE: Old World
Sparrows

House Sparrow (I) *
*Passer domesticus*

# Index of Birds

This index is of English names only. The last page for each species refers to the page in Appendix 1, A Checklist of Alabama and Mississippi Birds, where scientific order, family, genus, and species names are listed.

# Index of Locations

# NOTES

# NOTES